D0510707

100 15-MINUTE
FUSS-FREE RECIPES

100 15-MINUTE
FUSS-FREE RECIPES

Time-saving techniques and shortcuts to superb meals in minutes, including breakfasts, snacks, main course meat, fish and vegetarian dishes, plus dazzlingly simple desserts

Jenni Fleetwood

southwater

This edition is published by Southwater

Southwater is an imprint of Anness Publishing Ltd, Hermes House, 88–89 Blackfriars Road, London SE1 8HA; tel. 020 7401 2077; fax 020 7633 9499; www.southwaterbooks.com; www.annesspublishing.com

If you like the images in this book and would like to investigate using them for publishing, promotions or advertising, please visit our website www.practicalpictures.com for more information.

© Anness Publishing Ltd 2007

Ethical Trading Policy
Because of our ongoing ecological investment programme, you, as our customer, can have the pleasure and reassurance of knowing that a tree is being cultivated on your behalf to naturally replace the materials used to make the book you are holding. For further information about this scheme, go to www.annesspublishing.com/trees

UK agent: The Manning Partnership Ltd, 6 The Old Dairy, Melcombe Road, Bath BA2 3LR; tel. 01225 478444; fax 01225 478440; sales@manning-partnership.co.uk
UK distributor: Grantham Book Services Ltd, Isaac Newton Way, Alma Park Industrial Estate, Grantham, Lincs NG31 9SD; tel. 01476 541080; fax 01476 541061; orders@gbs.tbs-ltd.co.uk
North American agent/distributor: National Book Network, 4501 Forbes Boulevard, Suite 200, Lanham, MD 20706; tel. 301 459 3366; fax 301 429 5746; www.nbnbooks.com
Australian agent/distributor: Pan Macmillan Australia, Level 18, St Martins Tower, 31 Market St, Sydney, NSW 2000; tel. 1300 135 113; fax 1300 135 103; customer.service@macmillan.com.au
New Zealand agent/distributor: David Bateman Ltd, 30 Tarndale Grove, Off Bush Road, Albany, Auckland; tel. (09) 415 7664; fax (09) 415 8892

All rights reserved. No part of this publication may be reproduced, stored in a retrieval system, or transmitted in any way or by any means, electronic, mechanical, photocopying, recording or otherwise, without the prior written permission of the copyright holder.

A CIP catalogue record for this book is available from the British Library.

Previously published as part of a larger volume, *The 20-minute Cookbook*

Publisher: Joanna Lorenz
Editorial Director: Helen Sudell
Project Editor: Catherine Stuart
Production Controller: Wendy Lawson
Book Design: Diane Pullen and Michael Morey
Cover Design: Balley Design
Contributors: Pepita Aris, Mridula Baljekar, Jane Bamforth, Alex Barker, Judy Bastyra, Georgina Campbell, Coralie Dorman, Matthew Drennan, Joanna Farrow, Maria Filippelli, Jenni Fleetwood, Christine France, Brian Glover, Juliet Harbutt, Simona Hill, Becky Johnson, Bridget Jones, Lucy Knox, Jane Milton, Suzannah Olivier, Keith Richmond, Rena Salaman, Marlena Spieler, Liz Trigg, Linda Tubby, Sunil Vijayakar, Jenny White, Biddy White-Lennon, Kate Whiteman, Rosemary Wilkinson, Jeni Wright
Photography: Karl Adamson, Edward Allwright, Caroline Barty, Steve Baxter, Martin Brigdale, Nicki Dowey, James Duncan, Michelle Garrett, John Heseltine, Amanda Heywood, Janine Hosegood, Don Last, William Lingwood, Craig Robertson and Sam Stowell

Main front cover image shows Tofu and Green Bean Red Curry – for recipe, see page 91

3 5 7 9 10 8 6 4 2

Notes
Bracketed terms are intended for American readers.
For all recipes, quantities are given in both metric and imperial measures and, where appropriate, measures are also given in standard cups and spoons. Follow one set of measures, but not a mixture, because they are not interchangeable.
Standard spoon and cup measures are level. 1 tsp = 5ml, 1 tbsp = 15ml, 1 cup = 250ml/8fl oz.
Australian standard tablespoons are 20ml. Australian readers should use 3 tsp in place of 1 tbsp for measuring small quantities of gelatine, flour, salt etc.
American pints are 16fl oz/2 cups. American readers should use 20fl oz/2.5 cups in place of 1 pint when measuring liquids.
Electric oven temperatures in this book are for conventional ovens. When using a fan oven, the temperature will probably need to be reduced by about 10–20°C/20–40°F. Since ovens vary, you should check with your manufacturer's instruction book for guidance.
The nutritional analysis given for each recipe is calculated per portion (i.e. serving or item), unless otherwise stated. If the recipe gives a range, such as Serves 4–6, then the nutritional analysis will be for the smaller portion size, i.e. 6 servings.
Measurements for sodium do not include salt added to taste.
Medium eggs (US large) are used unless otherwise stated.

CONTENTS

GREAT FOOD FAST

Fifteen minutes isn't very long. You can easily spend that amount of time puzzling over a crossword clue, or trying to telephone a company determined to leave you on hold, or waiting for a cup of coffee in a busy restaurant. So can you cook a meal in 15 minutes? Yes you can, and this is the book to tell you how to do it.

When you want great food fast, what you need in your repertoire are easy, no-fuss recipes: breakfasts you can blitz in a blender; lunches you can prepare and pack in next to no time, and suppers that raise your spirits without sapping any of the energy you have left at the end of the day. You want food that looks as good as it tastes, but doesn't require you to carve a rose out of a radish. If you are entertaining, you want to do so in style, but without missing more than a few moments of your guests' company.

You can achieve these aims – after a fashion – by frequenting the ready meal section of your favourite supermarket. Some days you'll do just that, but it is much more rewarding and nutritious to serve something you've cooked yourself. Dishing up a ready meal is rather like reading a raunchy novel; satisfying as far as it goes, but sadly lacking as a sensory experience.

AN EXPERIENCE WORTH HAVING

Providing food need not be a chore. In fact, preparing a meal engages all of the senses. The glowing colours of the ingredients – a bunch of fresh basil, a bowl of tomatoes, a basket of vivid blueberries – are a delight to see. When you prepare them, your sense of touch comes into play. You cut a lemon or a lime, and immediately a lovely citrus aroma permeates the room. The pleasure continues with other satisfying smells: onions sizzling in a pan, apples and cloves simmering on the stove. With cooking smells come cooking sounds, and all help to stimulate the appetite. Before you take a single bite, you've already experienced a range of remarkable sensory experiences, and taste, the final food frontier, is still to come. Looked at that way, it isn't surprising that many of us love to cook, and would do much more of it if only we had the time.

PRESSING PRIORITIES

Time. There's the rub. We never seem to have enough of it. Whether you are a student, trying to balance study with a hectic social life, a single person trying to carve out a career or a parent with a different but equally pressing set of

Above: Ready-made dips and pâtés are often on the supermarket shopping list, but it's so easy to produce your own with just a few ingredients.

priorities, time is a precious luxury. We're all riding the rollercoaster, rushing from home to work to home to sport to parents' evening to home to sleep. Putting good food on the table should be in there somewhere, but sometimes it is difficult to achieve. That's why this book takes a pragmatic approach. Preparing your own vegetables is ideal, but if buying a bag of shake-it-out salad or some ready trimmed beans means you can eat well and still get to your night class, go for it. Look out for quick-cook versions of favourite ingredients, like polenta and rice, and don't be afraid of mixing bought items like pesto or tapenade with home-cooked pasta.

There is no longer any rule about precisely what constitutes a meal. You can have soup and a toasted sandwich one day, a stir-fry the next and a sophisticated treat like pan-fried steaks with whisky and cream on a Friday night. An everyday dish of grilled fish or meat can be enlivened by the easiest of touches, such as a dab of herb butter to melt over the top, or a simple sauce or salsa to serve on the side. There will be some occasions when you will want to offer a vegetable side dish, and others when the dish is so complete in itself that a chunk of bread is all that is

Left: This melt-in-the-mouth dish of Smoked Salmon and Chive Omelette is just one of many classic recipes that can be turned around in a few simple steps, and will never fail to delight.

Right: This dish of succulent pieces of chicken sautéed in lemon and garlic is just as suited to a last-minute weekday meal as when entertaining family and friends. Other meats such as turkey and pork will work just as well.

required. What matters is that you cook what you know you can cope with in the time available, and serve up something which everyone will enjoy.

THE RECIPES

The aim of this book is to provide a wide-ranging selection of recipes that can be cooked in 15 minutes or less. That's assuming the cook is reasonably experienced. If you've never chopped an onion in your life, it is likely to take you a little longer. Efficient cooking is all about organization, so do read through each chosen recipe carefully, assemble your ingredients and give some thought to strategy. If something has to go in the oven, switch it on to heat up before you do anything else; if you need to add grated cheese in Step 4, grate it straight away. The recipe methods do reflect

Below: A sudden craving for your favourite dessert – like this glorious Baked Pineapple Alaska – can be answered in fifteen minutes or less.

this, but you need to work within the bounds of your own ability, and within the confines of your own kitchen. If a recipe calls for a slotted spoon and you need to rummage under the sink for one, you could lose valuable time, so be as well prepared as possible. If you are inexperienced, the best way to start is to choose a short recipe of 15 minutes or less, or opt for something that needs no cooking at all, such as a salad. Also,

enlist aid when you can: having a child or partner line up ingredients can be a huge help during preparation.

Some of the recipes in this book, particularly those in need of marinating or chilling time, require some advance preparation. The timeline at the top of the recipe will make it clear when this is required, and there'll probably be some mention of the fact in the recipe introduction, so do watch out for this. In most cases, the recipe still won't take more than 15 minutes in total, but the preparation will be in stages and not all at the same time. There are times when advance preparation is an advantage – when you want to get some dinner party cooking out of the way early, for instance.

When you have extra time on your hands, consider making stock or a few sauces that can be frozen for later use. Then, when you are in a rush, you'll have the means to make a simple speedy meal that tastes great. You'll find recipes for these in the opening chapter. This section also features great ideas for quick and easy vegetable and grain accompaniments, from classics with a twist such as Apple and Thyme Mash, to versatile delights such as Soy and Sesame Noodles, which can also be eaten cold as a snack.

THE 15-MINUTE KITCHEN

Although having the right recipes gives you the best start when it comes to producing great food in the shortest possible time, there are some other criteria to consider. Every workman needs decent tools, and having a well-equipped kitchen will help you to make more efficient use of your time. This doesn't mean owning every new gadget on the market, but it is sensible to invest in good quality knives and pans, accurate measuring equipment, spoons and spatulas and a few well-chosen appliances. A food processor is just about essential these days, particularly when speed is a prime consideration, and you will also benefit from having a good hand-held electric beater. The quick cook also needs a heavy griddle pan — for cooking items like salmon, duck and vegetables — and a wok for the stir-fries that are central to swift cooking. It also helps to have a repertoire of simple sauces and stocks, which can be made in advance and kept in the freezer. Some of the recipes in this book suggest suitable accompaniments, but if you need more inspiration, you'll find it right here.

EQUIPMENT: PANS, CUTTING AND MEASURING

You don't need a kitchen full of equipment to be a spontaneous and versatile cook. It is quality, not quantity, that counts when you're preparing and cooking food, particularly when choosing essential pieces of equipment such as pans and knives. As long as you look after them, these items should last for many years so are well worth the investment. The following section guides you through the essential items that make cooking as simple and enjoyable as possible, and also offers suggestions on how to improvise if you don't have the right piece of equipment.

PANS AND BAKEWARE

Always choose good quality pans with a solid, heavy base because they retain heat better and are less likely to warp or buckle. Heatproof glass lids are useful because they allow you to check cooking progress without having to uncover the pan repeatedly.

Pans: small, medium and large

When cooking large quantities of food, such as pasta or rice that need to be boiled in a large amount of water, the bigger the pan the better. It does not matter whether the pan is non-stick, but it is useful to have heatproof handles and lids so that the pan can double as a large ovenproof cookpot. A medium pan is ideal for cooking sauces and similar mixtures. For these a non-stick pan is best; it will help to prevent thickened sauces sticking and burning. Washing-up will also be easier. The same guidelines apply to a small pan, which is ideal for small quantities.

Frying pan

Select a non-stick pan that is shallow enough, so that it is easy to slide a metal spatula into it. A pan with an ovenproof handle and lid can be placed in the oven as a shallow casserole dish, and under the grill (broiler).

Baking sheets

Having one or two non-stick baking sheets on hand in the kitchen is invaluable to the busy cook. They can be used for a multitude of tasks such as roasting hazelnuts, or they can be placed under full dishes in the oven to catch any drips if the mixture overflows. Choose good quality heavy baking sheets that will not buckle in the oven.

Roasting pan

As a quick cook you may only roast meat or vegetables occasionally, but when you do, a good, heavy roasting pan is essential. Choose a large pan; you will achieve better results if there is room for heat to circulate as the food cooks. Potatoes, for example, will not crisp well if they are crammed together in a small pan. Treat all pans with care to get maximum usage from them.

Below: Baking sheets are essential to the busy cook's kitchen – having more than one will mean several things can be roasted, baked or grilled at the same time.

CUTTING AND GRINDING

Chopping, slicing, cutting, peeling and grinding are all essential aspects of food preparation so it's important to have the right tools for the job.

Chopping boards

Essential in every kitchen, these can be made of wood or plastic. Wooden boards tend to be heavier and more stable, but they must be thoroughly scrubbed in hot soapy water and properly dried. Plastic boards are easier to clean and better for cutting meat, poultry and fish.

Knives: cook's, vegetable and serrated

When buying knives, choose the best ones you can afford. They should feel comfortable in your hand, so try several different types and practise a cutting action before you buy. You will

Left: It is wise to invest in three good quality pans of different sizes.

need three different knives. A cook's knife is a good multi-purpose knife. The blade is usually about 18cm/7in long, but you may find that you prefer a slightly longer or shorter blade. A vegetable knife is a small version of the cook's knife and is used for finer cutting. A large serrated knife is essential for slicing bread and ingredients such as tomatoes, which have a hard-to-cut skin compared to the soft flesh underneath. Store knives safely and securely, out of reach of young children.

Vegetable peelers

These can have a fixed or swivel blade. Both types will make quick work of peeling vegetables and fruit, with less waste than a small knife.

Graters

These come in various shapes and sizes. Box graters have several different cutting blades and are easy to handle. Microplane graters have razor-sharp blades that retain their sharp edges. It is worth investing in several of these, with different grating surfaces.

MEASURING EQUIPMENT

Accurate measuring equipment is essential, particularly when making breads and cakes, which need very precise quantities of ingredients.

Weighing scales

These are good for measuring dry ingredients. Digital scales are the most accurate but balance scales that use weights or a sliding weight are also a good choice. Spring scales with a scoop and dial are not usually as precise.

Measuring cups

Suitable for dry or liquid ingredients, these standard measures usually come in a set of separate cups for different fractions or portions of a full cup.

Measuring jug/pitcher

This is essential for liquids. A heatproof glass jug is useful because it allows hot liquids to be measured and makes it easy to check the quantity.

Left: The traditional box grater is solid, reliable and easy to handle – with several different grating blades.

Measuring spoons

Table cutlery varies in size, so a set of standard measuring spoons is extremely useful for measuring small quantities.

Looking after knives

Although it might seem contradictory, the sharper the knife, the safer it is to use. It takes far more effort to use a blunt knife and this often results in accidents. Try to get into the habit of sharpening your knives regularly, because the blunter they become, the more difficult they are to use and the longer it will take to sharpen them. Always wash knives carefully after use and dry them thoroughly to prevent discolouring or rusting.

Below: Compact kitchen utensils such as measuring jugs and cups are vital to the art of successful quick cooking.

EQUIPMENT: BLENDING, BAKING, GRIDDLING AND WOK-FRYING

MIXING, ROLLING AND DRAINING

Bowls, spoons, whisks and strainers are vital to the 15-minute kitchen. Establish suitable places to store the following equipment, so that you always know where to find it in a hurry. Having essentials to hand is one of the golden rules of successful quick cooking.

Mixing bowls

You will need one large and one small bowl. Heatproof glass bowls are a good choice because they can be placed over a pan of simmering water to heat delicate sauces and to melt chocolate.

Wooden spoons

Inexpensive and essential for stirring and beating, every kitchen should have two or three wooden spoons.

Metal slotted spoon

This large spoon with draining holes is very useful for lifting small pieces of food out of cooking liquid.

Fish slice/metal spatula

This is invaluable for lifting delicate fish fillets and other foods out of a pan.

Rolling pin

A heavy wooden or marble rolling pin is useful for rolling out pastry. If you don't have one, use a clean, dry, tall glass bottle (such as a wine bottle) instead.

Balloon whisk

A metal balloon whisk is great for softly whipping cream and whisking sauces to a smooth consistency. Whisks are available in all shapes and sizes. Do not buy an enormous whisk that is difficult to use and will not fit into pans. Mini-whisks are not essential – you can always use a fork instead.

Sieve/Strainer

For sifting flour, icing (confectioners') sugar, cocoa and other dry ingredients, a stainless-steel sieve is essential. It can also be used for straining small quantities of cooked vegetables, pasta and rice. Wash and dry a sieve well after use to prevent it becoming heavily clogged and damp.

Colander

Choose a free-standing metal colander with feet on the base. This has the advantage of leaving both hands free to empty heavy pans, and will keep the base of the colander above the liquid that is being drained off.

ELECTRICAL APPLIANCES

Although not always essential, these can speed up preparation.

Food processor

This fabulous invention can make life a lot easier. It is perfect for processing soft and hard foods and is more versatile than a blender, which is best suited to puréeing very soft foods or liquids.

Hand-held electric whisk

A small, hand-held electric whisk or beater is very useful for making cakes, whipping cream and whisking egg whites. Choose an appliance with sturdy beaters and a powerful motor that will last.

Above: Wooden spoons and spatulas are essential for stirring, beating and lifting.

Below: A food processor is the quick cook's best friend, especially if it has a mini bowl – perfect for grinding nuts or making breadcrumbs for toppings.

Above: Cookie cutters come in all kinds of shapes and sizes.

Above: A pastry brush is useful when baking or grilling (broiling).

EXTRA EQUIPMENT

As well as the essential items, some recipes require other items such as tart tins (pans) and cookie cutters. The following are some items you may find useful, whether you are putting together a speedy snack or attempting something more elaborate.

Cookie cutters

These make quick work of cutting out pastry and cookie dough. Metal ones have a sharper cutting edge so are usually preferable to plastic ones. If you don't have cutters, you can use a glass which is much quicker.

Pastry brush

Made of bristle, with a wooden or plastic handle, this is useful for brushing food lightly with liquid – for example, brushing meat or fish with oil or marinade while grilling (broiling).

CAKE TINS/PANS

These can have loose bottoms or spring-clip sides to allow easy removal of the cake. Be sure to use the size specified in the recipe.

Tartlet tins/muffin pans

These consist of six or twelve fairly deep cups in a tray. They can be used for baking tartlets, muffins, cupcakes, buns and bread rolls.

Tart tins/pans

Available with straight or fluted sides, these are not as deep as tartlet tins (muffin pans). They come in a variety of sizes, from individual containers to very large tins. They are useful for baking all kinds of sweet and savoury tarts. Loose-bottomed tins are best because they allow you to remove the contents more easily.

Skewers

These are used for kebabs and other skewered foods. Metal skewers are reusable and practical if you cook over the barbecue frequently, or cook kebabs that need lengthy cooking. Bamboo skewers are disposable and useful for foods that cook quickly – soak them in cold water before use to stop them burning.

Palette knife/metal spatula

Use this large, flat, round-bladed, blunt knife for spreading or flipping pancakes.

Griddle pan

A good quality, heavy griddle pan is useful for cooking meat and fish. The pan should be very hot before food is placed on it and you should brush the surface of the food with a little oil to prevent it from sticking, rather than adding oil to the pan. To clean, hot soapy water can be used but make sure the pan has cooled before washing, and then rinse and dry thoroughly. Do not plunge into water for soaking.

Above: A heavy griddle pan is a boon to the quick cook.

Wok

Larger and deeper than a frying pan, often with a rounded base, a wok has high sides and a large surface area, which make it ideal for stir-frying, steaming and simmering. Clean with hot water (no soap) and wipe with kitchen paper until the paper comes away clean.

Below: Woks come with one or two handles. The two-handled variety makes a good table centrepiece when dishing up a sizzling supper from wok to plate during a dinner party or family meal.

SIMPLE WAYS TO FLAVOUR FOOD

As well as selecting the cooking method best suited to the ingredients, there are several quick and simple methods of adding flavour using herbs, spices and aromatics. Match the seasoning to the ingredient and go for simple techniques such as marinating, stuffing or coating with a dry spice rub, which will help to intensify the flavours. The longer you leave food in a marinade or with a rub, the more the flavours will penetrate, so if you want to incorporate these techniques in a quick meal, you need to do a bit of forward planning.

FLAVOURS FOR FISH

Classic aromatics used for flavouring fish and shellfish include lemon, lime, parsley, dill, fennel and bay leaves. These flavours all have a fresh, intense quality that complements the delicate taste of fish and shellfish without overpowering it. All work well added before, during or after cooking, either as a filling or a marinade.

• To flavour whole fish, such as trout or mackerel, stuff a few lemon slices and some fresh parsley or basil into the body cavity before cooking. Season with plenty of salt and freshly ground black pepper, then wrap the fish in foil or baking parchment, ensuring the packet is well sealed. Place the fish in an ovenproof dish or on a baking tray and bake until cooked through.
• To make an unusual, yet delicious, marinade for salmon, arrange the salmon fillets in a single layer in an overproof dish. Drizzle the fillets with a little light olive oil and add a split vanilla pod. Cover and chill for a couple of hours before cooking.

• To marinate chunky fillets of fish, such as cod or salmon, arrange the fish fillets in a dish in a single layer. Drizzle the fish with olive oil, then sprinkle over a little crushed garlic and grated lime rind and squeeze over lime juice. Cover the dish in clear film (plastic wrap) and leave to marinate in the refrigerator for at least 30 minutes. Grill (broil) lightly until just cooked through.

PEPPING UP MEAT AND POULTRY

Meat and poultry can take both delicate and punchy seasonings. Dry rubs, marinades and sticky glazes are all perfect ways to introduce flavour into the food. Marinating the tougher cuts, such as stewing steak, also helps to make the meat more tender. A quick way of introducing flavour to meat is to inject it with marinade using a veterinary syringe.

• To make a fragrant Cajun spice rub for pork chops, steaks and chicken, mix together 5ml/1 tsp each dried thyme, dried oregano, finely crushed black peppercorns, salt, crushed cumin seeds and hot paprika. Rub the Cajun spice mix into the raw meat or poultry, then barbecue or bake until cooked.

• To marinate red meat, such as beef, lamb or venison, prepare a mixture of two-thirds red wine to one-third olive oil in a shallow non-metallic dish. Stir in some chopped garlic and bruised fresh rosemary sprigs. Add the meat and turn to coat it in the marinade. Cover and chill for at least 2 hours or overnight before cooking.
• To make a mildly-spiced sticky mustard glaze for chicken, pork or red meat, mix 45ml/3 tbsp each Dijon mustard, clear honey and demerara (raw) sugar, 2.5ml/½ tsp chilli powder, 1.5ml/¼ tsp ground cloves, and salt and ground black pepper. Cook the poultry or meat over the barbecue or under the grill (broiler) and brush with the glaze about 10 minutes before the end of the cooking time.
• A lemon grass and ginger marinade that can be whizzed up in the food processor is quick and easy and works well with chicken or pork. Chop the lower half of two lemon grass stalks and put them in the bowl of a food processor with 30ml/2 tbsp sliced fresh root ginger, 6 chopped garlic cloves, 4 chopped shallots, ½ bunch chopped coriander (cilantro) roots, 30ml/2 tbsp each Thai fish sauce and light soy sauce, 120ml/4fl oz/½ cup coconut milk and 1 tbsp palm sugar. Process until smooth, pour over 8 chicken portions and marinate for at least 4 hours. Bake the chicken pieces in the oven or cook over a barbecue, brushing them with the marinade once or twice during cooking.

Below: Brush on sticky glazes towards the end of the cooking time; if the glaze is cooked for too long, it will burn.

Above: Adding a drizzle of sesame oil to stir-fried vegetables gives them a wonderfully rich, smoky, nutty flavour.

VIBRANT VEGETABLES

Most fresh vegetables have a subtle flavour that needs to be brought out and enhanced. When using speedy cooking methods such as steaming and stir-frying, go for light, fresh flavourings that will enhance the taste of the vegetables. When using more robust cooking methods, such as roasting, choose richer flavours such as garlic and spices.

• To make fragrant, Asian-style steamed vegetables, add a bruised stalk of lemon grass and/or a few kaffir lime leaves to the steaming water, then cook vegetables such as pak choi (bok choy) over the water until just tender. Alternatively, place the aromatics in the steamer under the vegetables and steam as before until just tender.
• To add a rich flavour to stir-fried vegetables, add a splash of sesame oil just before the end of cooking time. (Do not use more than 5ml/1 tsp because sesame oil has a very strong flavour and can be overpowering.)

• To enhance the taste of naturally sweet vegetables, such as parsnips and carrots, glaze them with honey and mustard before roasting. Mix together 30ml/2 tbsp wholegrain mustard and 45ml/3 tbsp clear honey, and season with salt and ground black pepper. Brush the glaze over the prepared vegetables to coat completely, then roast until sweet and tender. To cut the roasting time, par-boil the vegetables first.

FRAGRANT RICE AND GRAINS

Classic accompaniments, such as rice and couscous, can be enhanced by the addition of simple flavourings. Adding herbs, spices and aromatics can help to perk up the rice and grains' subtle flavour without overpowering them. Always choose flavourings that will complement the dish with which the rice or grains will be served.

• To make exotic fragrant rice to serve with Asian-style stir-fries and braised dishes, add a whole star anise or a few cardamom pods to a pan of rice before cooking. The rice will absorb the flavour during cooking. Remove the spices from the pan using a slotted spoon just before serving the rice.

• To make zesty herb rice or couscous, heat a little chopped fresh tarragon and grated lemon rind in olive oil or melted butter until warm, then drizzle the flavoured oil and herbs over freshly cooked rice or couscous.

• To make simple fresh herb rice or couscous, fork plenty of chopped fresh parsley and chives through the cooked grains and drizzle over a little oil just before serving.

• Add roasted seeds to rice for a delicious flavour. Place 50g/2oz/6 tbsp mixed pumpkin seeds and sunflower seeds in a non-stick frying pan over a medium heat. Toss until golden, cool, and mix into cooked long grain rice.

BASICS: OILS, STOCKS, MARINADES AND DRESSINGS

Having a few ready-made basics, such as stocks, pasta sauces and flavoured oils, can really speed up everyday cooking. They can all be bought ready-made in the supermarket, but they are easy to make at home. Stocks take time to prepare, but they can be stored in the freezer for several months. Flavoured oils are straightforward and keep in the same way as ordinary oils so it's well worth having a few in the cupboard. All the basic sauces, dressings, marinades and flavoured creams on the following pages are simple to prepare and can either be made fresh or in advance.

FLAVOURED OILS

Good quality olive oil can be flavoured with herbs, spices and aromatics for drizzling, dressing and cooking.

Herb-infused oil

Half-fill a jar with washed and dried fresh herbs such as rosemary or basil. Pour over olive oil to cover, then seal the jar and place in a cool, dark place for 3 days. Strain the oil into a clean jar or bottle and discard the herbs.

Lemon oil

Finely pare the rind from one lemon, place on kitchen paper, and leave to dry for 1 day. Add the dried rind to a bottle of olive oil and leave to infuse for up to 3 days. Strain the oil into a clean bottle and discard the rind.

Chilli oil

Add several dried chillies to a bottle of olive oil and leave to infuse for about 2 weeks before using. If the flavour is

not sufficiently pronounced, leave for another week. The chillies can be left in the bottle and give a very decorative and colourful effect.

Garlic oil

Add several whole garlic cloves to a bottle of olive oil and leave to infuse for about 2 weeks before using. If the flavour is not sufficiently pronounced, leave the oil to infuse for another week, then strain the oil into a clean bottle and store in a cool, dark place.

STOCKS

When you have a little time on your hands, make stock. A supply of home-made stock in the freezer gives you the basis of dozens of quick and easy dishes, including risotto and a range of sauces. It's also a great way of using up leftover chicken, meat and fish, or a surplus of vegetables. To freeze, pour the cooled stock into 600ml/1 pint/2½ cup containers and freeze for up to 2 months.

Chicken stock

Put a 1.3kg/3lb chicken carcass into a large pan with 2 peeled and quartered onions, 2 halved carrots, 2 roughly chopped celery sticks, 1 bouquet garni, 1 peeled garlic clove and 5 black peppercorns. Pour in 1.2 litres/2 pints/ 5 cups cold water and bring to the boil. Reduce the heat, cover and simmer for 4–5 hours, regularly skimming off any scum from the surface and adding more water if needed. Strain the stock through a sieve (strainer) lined with kitchen paper and leave to cool.

Beef stock

Preheat the oven to 230°C/450°F/Gas 8. Put 1.8kg/4lb beef bones in a roasting pan and roast for 40 minutes, until browned, turning occasionally. Transfer the bones and vegetables to a large pan. Cover with water, add 2 chopped tomatoes and cook as for chicken stock.

Fish stock

Put 2 chopped onions, 1.3kg/3lb fish bones and heads, 300ml/½ pint/1¼ cups white wine, 5 black peppercorns and 1 bouquet garni in a large pan. Pour in 2 litres/3½ pints/9 cups water. Bring to the boil and simmer for 20 minutes, skimming often. Strain.

Vegetable stock

Put 900g/2lb chopped vegetables, including onions, leeks, tomatoes, carrots, parsnips and cabbage, in a large pan. Pour in 1.5 litres/2½ pints/ 6¼ cups water. Bring to the boil and simmer for 30 minutes, then strain.

MARINADES

These strong-tasting mixes are perfect for adding flavour to meat, poultry, fish and vegetables. Most ingredients should be marinated for at least 30 minutes.

Ginger and soy marinade

This is perfect for use with chicken and beef. Peel and grate a 2.5cm/1in piece of fresh root ginger and peel and finely chop a large garlic clove. In a small bowl, whisk 60ml/4 tbsp olive oil with 75ml/5 tbsp dark soy sauce. Season with ground black pepper and stir in the ginger and garlic.

Rosemary and garlic marinade

This is ideal for robust fish, lamb and chicken. Roughly chop the leaves from 3 fresh rosemary sprigs. Finely chop 2 garlic cloves and whisk with the rosemary, 75ml/5 tbsp olive oil and the juice of 1 lemon. Add the grated rind of the lemon too, if you like.

Lemon grass and lime marinade

Use this delicately-flavoured marinade with pieces of fish and chicken. Finely chop 1 lemon grass stalk. Whisk the grated rind and juice of 1 lime with 75ml/5 tbsp olive oil, salt and black pepper to taste, and the lemon grass.

Red wine and bay marinade

This easy-to-learn marinade is ideal for flavouring red meat, particularly if you want to soften the texture of tougher cuts. Whisk together 150ml/¼ pint/ ⅔ cup red wine, 1 finely chopped garlic clove, 2 torn fresh bay leaves and 45ml/3 tbsp olive oil. Season to taste with black pepper.

Below: Marinades containing red wine are particularly good for tenderizing tougher cuts of meat such as stewing steak.

DRESSINGS

Freshly made dressings are delicious drizzled over salads but are also tasty served with cooked vegetables and simply cooked fish, meat and poultry. You can make these dressings a few hours in advance and store them in a sealed container in the refrigerator until ready to use. Give them a quick whisk before drizzling over the food.

Honey and wholegrain mustard dressing

Drizzle this sweet, peppery dressing over leafy salads, fish, chicken and red meat dishes or toss with warm new potatoes. Whisk together 15ml/1 tbsp wholegrain mustard, 30ml/2 tbsp white wine vinegar, 15ml/1 tbsp honey and 75ml/5 tbsp extra virgin olive oil and season generously with salt and ground black pepper.

Orange and tarragon dressing

Serve this fresh, tangy dressing with salads and grilled (broiled) fish. In a small bowl, whisk the rind and juice of 1 large orange with 45ml/3 tbsp olive oil and 15ml/1 tbsp chopped fresh tarragon. Season with salt and plenty of ground black pepper to taste and chill before use if possible.

Toasted coriander and cumin dressing

Drizzle this warm, spicy dressing over grilled (broiled) chicken, lamb or beef. Heat a small frying pan and sprinkle in 15ml/1 tbsp each coriander and cumin seeds. Dry-fry until the seeds release their aromas and start to pop, then crush the seeds using a mortar and pestle. Add 45ml/3 tbsp olive oil, whisk to combine, then leave to infuse for 20 minutes. Season with salt and pepper to taste.

Lemon and horseradish dressing

This tangy dressing is particularly good with cooked beetroot. For a quick and easy lunch, serve it with smoked mackerel and a herb salad. There is no need to dress the salad – this delight-fully creamy relish will do very nicely sitting on the side of the plate. In a small bowl, combine 30ml/2 tbsp freshly squeezed lemon juice and 30ml/2 tbsp mirin or dry sherry. Whisk well, then add 120ml/4fl oz/½ cup olive oil, continuing to whisk the dressing until it emulsifies. Whisk in 30ml/2 tbsp creamed horseradish. Taste the dressing, and add a little salt and black pepper, if you think it needs it. The dressing should be smooth in texture.

BASICS: SAVOURY SAUCES AND DIPS

A repertoire of simple savoury sauce recipes is a must for the versatile quick cook. The following suggestions can be stirred through pasta and grains, heaped on baked potatoes, used to add interest to simple grilled (broiled) meats or fish, or served as savoury dips.

SAVOURY SAUCES

The following classic sauces can be made in a matter of minutes, and are so much nicer than their ready-bought counterparts. You'll need a blender for the pesto variations.

Easy tomato sauce

Toss with pasta, top a pizza or serve with fish and chicken. Heat 15ml/1 tbsp olive oil in a pan, add 1 chopped onion and fry for 2–3 minutes until soft. Add 1 chopped garlic clove and cook for 1 minute more. Pour in 400g/14oz chopped canned tomatoes and stir in 15ml/1 tbsp tomato purée (paste). Add 30ml/2 tbsp dried oregano and simmer for 15 minutes, until thickened. Season.

Quick satay sauce

Serve this spicy Asian-style sauce with grilled (broiled) chicken, beef or prawns (shrimp), or toss with freshly cooked egg noodles. Put 30ml/2 tbsp crunchy peanut butter in a pan and stir in 150ml/¼ pint/⅔ cup coconut milk, 45ml/3 tbsp hot water, a pinch of chilli powder and 30ml/2 tbsp light soy sauce. Heat gently, stirring until the peanut butter has melted and the mixture is well blended. Simmer for about a minute and serve immediately, while still hot.

Mustard cheese sauce

Stir this sauce through pasta, or serve with vegetables or baked white fish. Melt around 25g/1oz/2 tbsp butter in a medium pan and stir in 25g/1oz/¼ cup plain (all-purpose) flour. Remove the pan from the heat and stir in 5ml/1 tsp prepared English mustard.

Gradually add 200ml/7fl oz/scant 1 cup milk, stirring well to remove any lumps. (If the sauce becomes lumpy, whisk until smooth.) Return the pan to the heat and bring to the boil, stirring constantly. Remove from the heat and stir in 115g/4oz/1 cup grated Gruyère or Cheddar cheese. Continue to blend, away from the heat, until the cheese has melted and the texture is smooth. Season to taste.

Traditional pesto

This classic Italian sauce is made with basil, garlic, pine nuts and Parmesan cheese but there are many variations. Toss with pasta, stir into mashed potatoes or plain boiled rice, or use to flavour sauces and dressings. Put 50g/2oz fresh basil leaves in a food processor and blend to a paste with 25g/1oz/¼ cup toasted pine nuts and 2 peeled garlic cloves. With the motor still running, drizzle in 120ml/4fl oz/½ cup extra virgin olive oil until the mixture forms a paste. Spoon the pesto into a bowl and stir in 25g/1oz/⅓ cup freshly grated Parmesan cheese. Season to taste with salt and ground black pepper.

Parsley and walnut pesto

Put 50g/2oz fresh parsley leaves in a food processor and blend to a paste with 25g/1oz/¼ cup walnuts and 2 peeled garlic cloves. With the motor still running, drizzle in 120ml/4fl oz/½ cup extra virgin olive oil until the mixture forms a paste. Spoon the pesto into a bowl and stir in 25g/1oz/⅓ cup freshly grated Parmesan cheese. Season to taste with salt and ground black pepper.

Rocket pesto

Put 50g/2oz fresh rocket (arugula) leaves into a food processor and blend to a paste with 25g/1oz/¼ cup toasted pine nuts and 2 peeled garlic cloves. With the motor still running, drizzle in 120ml/4fl oz/½ cup extra virgin olive oil until the mixture forms a paste. Spoon the pesto into a bowl and stir in 25g/1oz/⅓ cup freshly grated Parmesan cheese. Season to taste with salt and ground black pepper.

Asian-style pesto

Try this Asian version of Italian pesto tossed with freshly cooked egg noodles. Put 50g/2oz fresh coriander (cilantro) leaves into a food processor and add 25g/1oz/¼ cup toasted pine nuts, 2 peeled garlic cloves and 1 seeded and roughly chopped green chilli. Blend until smooth. With the motor still running, drizzle in 120ml/4fl oz/½ cup extra virgin olive oil until the mixture forms a paste. Spoon the pesto into a bowl and season to taste with salt and ground black pepper.

Coriander and pistachio pesto

This aromatic pesto is delicious over fish or chicken. Put 50g/2oz fresh coriander (cilantro) leaves in a food processor. Add 15g/½oz fresh parsley and process until finely chopped. Add 2 seeded and chopped fresh red chillies, and 1 garlic clove. Process until finely chopped.

Add 50g/2oz/⅓ cup shelled pistachio nuts and pulse until roughly chopped. Stir in 25g/1oz/⅓ cup grated Parmesan cheese, 90ml/6 tbsp olive oil and the juice of 2 limes. Season with salt and pepper to taste.

SAVOURY DIPS

These richly flavoured dips are delicious served with tortilla chips, crudités or small savoury crackers, but can also be served as an accompaniment to grilled (broiled) or poached chicken and fish. The creamy dips also make flavourful dressings for salads; you may need to thin them slightly with a squeeze of lemon juice or a little cold water.

Blue cheese dip

This sharp, tangy mixture is best served with crudites. Put 200ml/7fl oz/scant 1 cup crème fraîche in a large bowl and add 115g/4oz/1 cup crumbled blue cheese such as Stilton. Stir well until the mixture is smooth and creamy. Season with salt and ground black pepper and fold in about 30ml/2 tbsp chopped fresh chives.

Sour cream and chive dip

This tasty dip is a classic combination and goes particularly well with crudités and savoury crackers. Put 200ml/7fl oz/scant 1 cup sour cream in a bowl and add 30ml/2 tbsp chopped fresh chives and a pinch of caster (superfine) sugar. Stir well to mix, then season with salt and ground black pepper.

Classic mayonnaise

There are some excellent makes of mayonnaise on the market and these are what you'll reach for when time is short. However, for that special-occasion meal, nothing beats home-made mayonnaise. Surprisingly, it doesn't take much longer to make than spooning the bought stuff out of the jar. Put 2 egg yolks, 10ml/2 tsp lemon juice, 5ml/1 tsp Dijon mustard and some salt and ground black pepper in a food processor. Process briefly to combine, then, with the motor running, drizzle in about 350ml/12fl oz/1½ cups olive oil. The mayonnaise will become thick and pale. Scrape the mayonnaise into a bowl, taste and add more lemon juice and salt and pepper if necessary.

Aioli

This classic French garlic mayonnaise is particularly good served with piping hot chips (French fries). Make the mayonnaise as described above, adding 2 peeled garlic cloves to the food processor with the egg yolks.

Lemon or caper mayonnaise

A tangy mayonnnaise complements cold poached fish perfectly. Make the mayonnaise as described above, adding the grated rind of 1 lemon to the food processor with the egg yolks. For caper mayonnaise, simply add 15ml/1 tbsp rinsed capers instead of the lemon zest.

Herb mayonnaise

Finely chop a handful of fresh herbs, such as basil, coriander (cilantro) and tarragon, and stir into freshly made plain mayonnaise.

BASICS: FRUIT RELISHES, SWEET SAUCES AND FLAVOURED CREAMS

Tart fruit sauces and relishes are the perfect foil to fish, poultry and pork, as they nicely offset rich flavours and oily textures. The avocado salsa, laced with the juice of a lime, works well as an accompaniment to corn snacks, but is also delicious served on the side with pork, poultry or steak. After sampling these fruity flavours, move on to sheer indulgence with an irresistible selection of dessert sauces and creams. Sweetness is supplied by spices, syrups, soft fruits, chocolate and fortified wines.

Apple sauce

Serve with pork. Peel, core and slice 450g/1lb cooking apples and place in a pan. Add a splash of water, 15ml/1 tbsp caster (superfine) sugar and a few whole cloves. Cook the apples over a gentle heat, stirring occasionally, until the fruit becomes pulpy.

Quick cranberry sauce

Serve with roast chicken or turkey. Put 225g/8oz/2 cups cranberries in a pan with about 75g/3oz/scant ½ cup light muscovado (brown) sugar, 45ml/3 tbsp port and 45ml/3 tbsp orange juice. Bring to the boil, then simmer, uncovered, for 10 minutes, or until the cranberries are tender. Stir occasionally to stop the fruit from sticking.

Gooseberry relish

Serve this tart relish with oily fish, such as mackerel, or fatty meat such as pork. Put 225g/8oz fresh or frozen gooseberries in a pan with 225g/8oz/ generous 1 cup caster (superfine) sugar and 1 star anise. Add a splash of water

and a little white wine if you like. Bring to the boil and simmer, uncovered, for 10 minutes, stirring occasionally, until the fruit has broken down and the texture is soft and pulpy.

Avocado and cumin salsa

Serve this spicy Mexican-style salsa as an unusual accompaniment to a meat meal, or solo, with a large bowl of tortilla chips. They're the perfect shape for scooping up the chunky salsa. Peel, stone (pit) and roughly chop 1 ripe avocado. Transfer to a bowl and gently stir in 1 finely chopped fresh red chilli, 15ml/1 tbsp toasted crushed cumin seeds, 1 chopped ripe tomato, the juice of 1 lime, 45ml/3 tbsp olive oil and 30ml/2 tbsp chopped fresh coriander (cilantro). Season and serve.

SWEET SAUCES

These luscious sauces are perfect spooned over ice cream and can turn a store-bought dessert or slice of sponge cake into an indulgent treat.

White chocolate sauce

Break 150g/5oz white chocolate into squares. Heat 150ml/¼ pint/⅔ cup double (heavy) cream in a heavy pan. When almost boiling, stir in the white chocolate, a few pieces at a time, until melted and smooth. Remove from the heat and stir in 30ml/2 tbsp brandy or Cointreau. Serve the sauce hot.

Toffee chocolate sauce

This is perhaps the simplest sweet sauce to make of all. Roughly chop 2 Mars bars (chocolate toffee bars) and

put the pieces in a pan with 300ml/ ½ pint/1¼ cups double (heavy) cream. Stir over a gentle heat until the chocolate bars have melted. Serve hot with ice cream, or combine with 50g/2oz/1 cup corn flakes to make chocolate crispy cakes.

Raspberry and vanilla sauce

Scrape the seeds from a vanilla pod (bean) into a food processor. Add 175g/ 6oz/1 cup raspberries and 30ml/2 tbsp icing (confectioners') sugar. Process to a purée, adding a little water to thin, if necessary.

Chocolate fudge sauce

Put 175ml/6fl oz/¾ cup double (heavy) cream in a small pan with 45ml/3 tbsp golden (light corn) syrup, 200g/7oz/ scant 1 cup light muscovado (brown) sugar and a pinch of salt. Heat gently, stirring, until the sugar has dissolved. Add 75g/3oz/½ cup chopped plain (semisweet) chocolate and stir until melted. Simmer the sauce gently for about 20 minutes, stirring occasionally, until thickened. Keep warm in a heatproof bowl until ready to use.

FLAVOURED CREAMS

Cream is the perfect accompaniment for any dessert – whether it's a healthy fruit salad, a sumptuous plum tart or a warming baked apple. Flavoured creams are even better and can transform a tasty dessert into a truly luscious one.

Rosemary and almond cream

This fragrant cream has a lovely texture and is good served with fruit compotes, pies and tarts. Pour 300ml/½ pint/1¼ cups double (heavy) cream into a pan and add 2 fresh rosemary sprigs. Heat the mixture until just about to boil, then remove the pan from the heat and leave the mixture to infuse for 20 minutes. Remove the rosemary from the pan and discard. Pour the cream into a bowl and chill until cold. Whip the cold cream into soft peaks and stir in 30ml/2 tbsp chopped toasted almonds.

Rum and cinnamon cream

You can serve this versatile cream with most desserts. It goes particularly well with coffee, chocolate and fruit. Pour 300ml/½ pint/1¼ cups double (heavy) cream into a pan and add a cinnamon stick. Heat the mixture until it is just about to boil, then remove the pan from the heat and leave to infuse for about 20 minutes. Strain the cream through a fine sieve (strainer) and place in the refrigerator until cold. Whip the cold cream until it stands in soft peaks, then stir in 30ml/2 tbsp rum and 15ml/1 tbsp icing (confectioners') sugar, sifted if necessary, until thoroughly combined. Try a variation with 30ml/2 tbsp advocaat liqueur and 15ml/1 tbsp ginger conserve, too.

Marsala mascarpone

This sweet cream, based on a rich Italian cheese, is perfect for serving with grilled (broiled) fruit, tarts and hot desserts. Spoon 200g/7oz/scant 1 cup mascarpone into a large bowl and add 30ml/2 tbsp icing (confectioners') sugar and 45ml/3 tbsp Marsala. Beat the mixture until smooth. Another alcohol and sweet cream combo uses 45ml/3 tbsp Amaretto to 300ml/½ pint/1¼ cups whipped cream. Stir in 15ml/1 tbsp icing (confectioner's) sugar.

Cardamom cream

Warm, spicy cardamom pods make a wonderfully subtle, aromatic cream that is delicious served with fruit salads, compôtes, tarts and pies. It goes particularly well with tropical fruits such as mango. Pour 300ml/½ pint/1¼ cups double (heavy) cream into a pan and add 3 green cardamom pods. Heat the mixture gently until just about to boil, then remove the pan from the heat and leave to infuse for about 20 minutes. Pour the cream through a fine sieve (strainer) and place in the refrigerator until cold. Whip the cold cream until it stands in soft peaks, spoon it into a bowl and serve.

Praline cream

What could be more delicious than golden almond nut brittle, tasting of toffee but with a hint of bitterness from the nuts, blended with whipped cream? This is very good with poached apricots.

1 Put 115g/4oz/½ cup sugar and 75ml/5 tbsp water in a small, heavy pan. Stir over a gentle heat until the sugar has dissolved, then boil without stirring until the syrup is golden.

2 Remove from the heat, stir in 50g/2oz/⅓ cup whole blanched almonds and spread out on a lightly oiled baking sheet. Leave the nut syrup to cool until it turns glassy.

3 Scrape the hardened nut mixture off the surface of the baking tray and break into smaller pieces using your fingers, then put in a food processor. Process for about 1 minute, until finely chopped with the appearance of ground nuts.

4 In a large bowl, whip 300ml/½ pint/1¼ cups double (heavy) cream into soft peaks, then stir in the praline and serve immediately.

MAKING SIMPLE ACCOMPANIMENTS

When you've made a delicious main dish, you need to serve it with equally tasty accompaniments. The following section is full of simple, speedy ideas for fabulous side dishes – from creamy mashed potatoes, fragrant rice and spicy noodles to Italian-style polenta and simple, healthy vegetables.

MASHED POTATOES

Potatoes go well with just about any main dish. They can be cooked simply – boiled, steamed, fried or baked – but they are even better mashed with milk and butter.

Perfect mashed potatoes

Peel 675g/1½lb floury potatoes and cut them into large chunks. Place in a pan of salted boiling water. Return to the boil, then simmer for 15–20 minutes, or until completely tender. Drain the potatoes and return to the pan. Leave over a low heat for a couple of minutes, shaking the pan to drive off any excess moisture. Take the pan off the heat and, using a potato masher, mash the potatoes until smooth. Beat in 45–60ml/ 3–4 tbsp warm milk and a large knob (pat) of butter, then season with salt and pepper to taste.

Mustard mash

Make the mashed potatoes as directed above, then stir in 15–30ml/1–2 tbsp wholegrain mustard just before seasoning, and beat until smooth.

Parmesan and parsley mash

Make mashed potatoes as above, then stir in 30ml/2 tbsp freshly grated Parmesan and 15ml/1 tbsp chopped fresh flat leaf parsley.

Apple and thyme mash

Serve with pork. Make mashed potatoes as above. Heat 25g/1oz/2 tbsp butter in a pan and add 2 peeled, cored and sliced eating apples. Fry for 4–5 minutes, turning them often. Roughly mash, then fold into the potatoes, with 15ml/1 tbsp fresh thyme leaves.

Pesto mash

This is a simple way to dress up plain mashed potatoes. They have real bite and a lovely green-specked appearance. Make mashed potatoes as described above, then stir in 30ml/2 tbsp pesto sauce until thoroughly combined.

Masala mash

This tastes great with grilled (broiled) duck or pork. Put 15ml/1 tbsp mixed chopped fresh mint and coriander (cilantro) in a bowl. Add 5ml/1 tsp mango chutney, then stir in 5ml/1 tsp salt and 5ml/1 tsp crushed black peppercorns. Finely chop 1 fresh red and 1 fresh green chilli, removing the seeds if you like, and add to the mixture. Beat in 50g/2oz/¼ cup softened butter. Beat most of the herb mixture into the mashed potatoes and spoon the rest on top.

CRUSHED POTATOES

This chunky, modern version of mashed potatoes tastes fabulous. For all variations, simply crush the potatoes roughly, using the back of a fork.

Crushed potatoes with parsley and lemon

Cook 675g/1½lb new potatoes in salted boiling water for 15–20 minutes, until tender. Drain the potatoes and crush. Stir in 30ml/2 tbsp extra virgin olive oil, the grated rind and juice of 1 lemon and 30ml/2 tbsp chopped fresh flat leaf parsley. Season to taste.

Crushed potatoes with garlic and basil

Cook 675g/1½lb new potatoes in a pan of boiling salted water for 15–20 minutes until tender. Drain and crush. Stir in 30ml/2 tbsp extra virgin olive oil, 2 finely chopped garlic cloves and a handful of torn basil leaves. Season.

Crushed potatoes with pine nuts and Parmesan

Cook 675g/1½lb new potatoes in boiling salted water for 15–20 minutes until tender. Drain and crush. Stir in 30ml/ 2 tbsp extra virgin olive oil, 30ml/2 tbsp grated Parmesan cheese and 30ml/ 2 tbsp toasted pine nuts.

RICE

This versatile grain can be served simply – either boiled or steamed – or can be flavoured or stir-fried with different ingredients to make tasty, exciting accompaniments.

Easy egg-fried rice

Cook 115g/4oz/generous ½ cup long grain rice in a large pan of boiling water for 10–12 minutes, until tender. Drain well and refresh under cold running water. Spread out on a baking sheet and leave until completely cold. Heat 30ml/2 tbsp sunflower oil in a large frying pan and add 1 finely chopped garlic clove. Cook for 1 minute, then add the rice and stir-fry for 1 minute. Push the rice to the side of the pan and pour 1 beaten egg into the pan. Cook the egg until set, then break up with a fork and stir into the rice. Add a splash of soy sauce, and mix well.

Coconut rice

Put 225g/8oz/generous 1 cup basmati rice in a pan and pour in a 400ml/14oz can coconut milk. Cover with water, add some salt and bring to the boil. Simmer for 12 minutes, or until the rice is tender. Drain well and serve.

Coriander and spring onion rice

Cook 225g/8oz/generous 1 cup basmati rice in a large pan of salted boiling water for about 12 minutes, or until tender. Drain the rice well and return to the pan. Stir in 3 finely sliced spring onions (scallions) and a roughly chopped bunch of fresh coriander (cilantro) until well mixed, then serve.

NOODLES

There are many different types of noodles, all of which are quick to cook and make the perfect accompaniment to Chinese- and Asian-style stir-fries and curries. Serve them on their own, or toss them with a few simple flavourings. They can also be served cold as a simple salad.

Soy and sesame egg noodles

Cook a 250g/9oz packet of egg noodles according to the instructions on the packet. Drain well and tip the noodles into a large bowl. Drizzle over 30ml/ 2 tbsp dark soy sauce and 10ml/2 tsp sesame oil, then sprinkle over 15ml/ 1 tbsp toasted sesame seeds and toss well until thoroughly combined. These noodles will be delicious whether served hot, or cold as a salad.

Spicy peanut noodles

This simple and very tasty dish takes only minutes to make and is good on its own or with grilled (broiled) chicken. Cook a 250g/9oz packet of egg noodles according to the instructions on the packet, then drain. Heat 15ml/1 tbsp sunflower oil in a wok and add 30ml/ 2 tbsp crunchy peanut butter. Add a splash of cold water and a dash of soy sauce and stir the mixture over a gentle heat until thoroughly combined. Add the noodles to the pan and toss to coat in the peanut mixture. Sprinkle with fresh coriander (cilantro) to serve.

Chilli and spring onion noodles

Soak 115g/4oz flat rice noodles in cold water for 30 minutes, until softened. Tip into a colander and drain well. Heat 30ml/2 tbsp olive oil in a wok or large frying pan. Add 2 finely chopped garlic cloves and 1 seeded and finely chopped fresh red chilli and fry gently for 2 minutes. Slice a bunch of spring onions (scallions) and add to the pan. Cook for a minute or so, then stir in the rice noodles, combining them with the other ingredients until heated through. Season with salt and ground black pepper before serving.

POLENTA

This classic Italian dish made from cornmeal makes a swift and delicious accompaniment to many dishes and is a useful alternative to the usual potatoes, bread or pasta. It can be served in two ways – either soft, or set and cut into wedges and grilled (broiled) or fried. Soft polenta is rather like mashed potato, and like mashed potato, it can be layered with other ingredients and baked, or used as a topping. Grilled or fried polenta has a much firmer texture and a lovely crisp shell. Both types can be enjoyed plain, if you choose, or flavoured with other ingredients such as cheese, herbs and spices. Traditional polenta requires lengthy boiling and constant attention during cooking, but the quick-cook varieties, which are widely available in most large supermarkets, give excellent results and are much simpler and quicker to prepare.

Soft polenta

Cook 225g/8oz/2 cups quick-cook polenta according to the instructions on the packet. As soon as the polenta is cooked, stir in about 50g/2oz/¼ cup butter. Season with salt and black pepper to taste, then serve immediately.

Soft polenta with Parmesan and sage

Cook 225g/8oz/2 cups quick-cook polenta according to the instructions on the packet. As soon as the polenta is cooked, stir in 115g/4oz/1⅓ cups freshly grated Parmesan cheese and a handful of chopped fresh sage. Stir in a large knob (pat) of butter and season with salt and ground black pepper to taste before serving.

Soft polenta with Cheddar cheese and thyme

Cook 225g/8oz/2 cups quick-cook polenta according to the instructions on the packet. As soon as the polenta is cooked, stir in 50g/2oz/½ cups grated Cheddar cheese and 30ml/2 tbsp chopped fresh thyme until thoroughly combined. Stir a large knob (pat) of butter into the cheesy polenta and season with salt and plenty of ground black pepper to taste before serving.

Fried chilli polenta triangles

Cook 225g/8oz/2 cups quick-cook polenta according to the instructions on the packet. Stir in 5ml/1 tsp dried chilli flakes, check the seasoning, adding more if necessary, and spread the mixture out on an oiled baking sheet to a thickness of about 1cm/½in. Leave the polenta until cold and completely set, then chill for about 20 minutes. Turn the polenta out on to a board and cut it into large squares, then cut each square into 2 triangles. Heat 30ml/ 2 tbsp olive oil in a large frying pan. Fry the triangles in the olive oil for 2–3 minutes on each side, until golden, then lift out and drain briefly on kitchen paper before serving.

Grilled polenta with Gorgonzola

Cook 225g/8oz/2 cups quick-cook polenta according to the instructions on the packet. Check the seasoning, adding more if necessary, and spread the mixture out on an oiled baking sheet to a thickness of about 1cm/½in. Leave the polenta until cold and completely set, then chill for about 20 minutes. Turn the polenta out on to a board and cut it into large squares, then cut each square into 2 triangles. Pre-heat the grill (broiler) and arrange the polenta triangles on the grill pan. Cook for about 5 minutes, or until golden brown, then turn over and top each triangle with a sliver of Gorgonzola. Grill (broil) for a further 5 minutes, or until bubbling.

Baked polenta with two cheeses

Serve this simple bake with slices of prosciutto and a simple leaf and herb salad tossed with a lemon and honey dressing. Preheat the oven to 200°C/ 400°F/Gas 6. Grate 115g/4oz Cheddar cheese and crumble 115g/4oz soft Dolcelatte cheese. Mix the cheeses together in a bowl, using your fingers to combine them thoroughly. Cook 225g/8oz/2 cups quick-cook polenta according to the instructions on the packet. Spoon half the polenta into a baking dish and level the surface. Cover with half the cheese mixture, spoon the remaining polenta on top and sprinkle with the remaining cheese. Melt 50g/2oz/¼ cup butter in a pan and fry 2 chopped garlic cloves and a few chopped fresh sage leaves until golden. Drizzle over the polenta and grind black pepper over the top. Bake for 5 minutes until the cheese topping is bubbling.

QUICK AND SIMPLE VEGETABLES

Fresh vegetables are an essential part of our diet. They are delicious cooked on their own but they can also be combined with other ingredients.

Stir-fried cabbage with nuts and smoky bacon

Heat 30ml/2 tbsp sunflower oil in a wok or large frying pan and add 4 roughly chopped rashers (strips) smoked streaky (fatty) bacon. Stir-fry for about 3 minutes, until the bacon starts to turn golden, then add ½ shredded green cabbage to the pan. Stir-fry for 3–4 minutes, until the cabbage is just tender. Season with salt and ground black pepper, and stir in 25g/1oz/¼ cup roughly chopped toasted hazelnuts or almonds just before serving.

Creamy stir-fried Brussels sprouts

Shred 450g/1lb Brussels sprouts and add to the pan. Heat 15ml/1 tbsp sunflower oil in a wok or large frying pan. Add 1 chopped garlic clove and stir-fry for about 30 seconds. Stir-fry for 3–4 minutes, until just tender. Season with salt and black pepper and stir in 30ml/2 tbsp crème fraîche. Warm through for 1 minute.

Honey-fried parsnips and celeriac

Peel 225g/8oz parsnips and 115g/4oz celeriac. Cut both into matchsticks. Heat 30ml/2 tbsp olive oil in a wok or large frying pan and add the parsnips and celeriac. Fry over a gentle heat for 6–7 minutes, stirring occasionally, until golden and tender. Season with salt and ground black pepper and stir in 15ml/ 1 tbsp clear honey. Allow to bubble for 1 minute before serving.

Glazed carrots

Clear honey is the magic ingredient to use with this carrot side dish too. Cut three large carrots into matchsticks. Steam them over a pan of boiling water for 2–4 minutes until just tender. Meanwhile, heat 25g/1oz/2 tbsp butter in a heavy pan, add 1 crushed garlic clove and 15ml/1 tbsp chopped fresh rosemary leaves and cook for 1 minute or until the garlic is golden brown. Add 5ml/1 tsp Dijon mustard and 10ml/2 tsp clear honey. Stir over the heat until the honey has melted into the buttery sauce, then add the carrots. Cook, tossing the carrots to coat them with the mixture, for 2 minutes until the carrots are glazed. Season lightly with salt, if needed, and serve immediately.

SPECIALIST BREADS

Bread makes a simple accompaniment to many meals and is the perfect ready-made side dish when time is short. Look out for part-baked breads that you can finish off in the oven, so you can enjoy the taste of freshly baked bread in just a few minutes.

Ciabatta This chewy Italian bread is long and oval in shape and is commonly available in ready-to-bake form. Look out for ciabatta with added sun-dried tomatoes or olives.

Focaccia This flat, dimpled Italian bread is made with olive oil and has a softer texture than ciabatta. It is available plain but is also often flavoured with fresh rosemary and garlic.

Naan Traditionally cooked in a clay oven, this Indian bread is easy to find in supermarkets and makes a tasty accompaniment to curries. It is available plain, and also flavoured with spices.

Chapati This Indian flatbread is less heavy than naan and makes a good alternative. The small, round breads can be a little more difficult to find but are worth searching for.

Soda bread This traditional Irish bread is made using buttermilk and bicarbonate of soda (baking soda). It has a delicious flavour and is great for mopping up sauces or serving with soups.

Above: Rosemary focaccia has a crumbly texture and is perfect for sandwiches and for serving with a whole range of Italian-style dishes.

BREAKFASTS AND BRUNCHES

Early mornings are the busiest time. Something has to give, and all too often that something is breakfast. Nutritionists tell us how important this first meal of the day is, but still we skip it, or settle for coffee and a doughnut when the mayhem has moderated. Not a good idea. With just a few minutes to spare, you can make a delicious smoothie or a simple fruit compote. Pineapple, Ginger and Carrot Juice will give you plenty of zing, and get you off to a good start. Once you find out how good breakfast makes you feel, you'll want to revisit old favourites like Cinnamon Toast or Griddled Tomatoes on Soda Bread. When the weekend arrives and life is just a little less hectic, celebrate by making a special brunch. This is a great meal for sharing with friends. Whatever you choose to cook won't take long, thanks to our quick and easy recipes, so you'll soon be joining the party and accepting praise for your delectable Panettone French Toast or Sweet Breakfast Omelette.

PINEAPPLE, GINGER AND CARROT JUICE

YOU'RE NEVER TOO BUSY FOR BREAKFAST WHEN YOU HAVE RECIPES LIKE THIS ONE IN YOUR REPERTOIRE. GINGER ADDS A ZING TO THE SWEET, SCENTED MIXTURE OF FRESH PINEAPPLE AND CARROT. SERVED VERY COLD, THIS REFRESHING DRINK MAKES THE PERFECT START TO THE DAY.

Preparation: 5 minutes; Cooking: 0 minutes

MAKES ONE GLASS

INGREDIENTS
   ½ small pineapple
   25g/1oz fresh root ginger
   1 carrot
   ice cubes

COOK'S TIP
This is one of the speediest breakfast snacks there is, but you can prepare it even more quickly if you buy ready-sliced fresh pineapple. This is sold in tubs and you will often find it in the chiller at the local supermarket.

1 Using a sharp knife, cut away the skin from the pineapple, then cut it into quarters and remove the core from each piece. Roughly slice the pineapple flesh and then chop into portions small enough to fit in the juicer.

2 Thinly peel the ginger, using a sharp knife or vegetable peeler, then chop the flesh roughly. Scrape or peel the carrot and cut it into rounds or chunks.

3 Push the carrot, ginger and pineapple through a juicer and pour into a glass. Add ice cubes and serve immediately.

Energy 108kcal/462kJ; Protein 1.3g; Carbohydrate 26.1g, of which sugars 25.8g; Fat 0.6g, of which saturates 0.1g; Cholesterol 0mg; Calcium 55mg; Fibre 4.2g; Sodium 23mg

VITALITY JUICE

THE CLUE IS IN THE NAME. THIS SPEEDY JUICE REALLY DOES PUT A SPRING IN YOUR STEP. WATERCRESS HAS A SLIGHTLY PEPPERY FLAVOUR WHEN EATEN ON ITS OWN, BUT BLENDING IT WITH PEAR, WHEATGERM AND YOGURT TAMES THE TASTE WHILE BOOSTING YOUR MORNING ENERGY LEVELS.

Preparation: 4 minutes; Cooking: 0 minutes

SERVES ONE

INGREDIENTS
    25g/1oz watercress
    1 large ripe pear
    30ml/2 tbsp wheatgerm
    150ml/¼ pint/⅔ cup natural
      (plain) yogurt
    15ml/1 tbsp linseeds (flax seeds)
    10ml/2 tsp lemon juice
    mineral water (optional)
    ice cubes

1 Roughly chop the watercress (you do not need to remove the tough stalks). Peel, core and roughly chop the pear.

2 Put the watercress and pear in a blender or food processor with the wheatgerm and blend until smooth. Scrape the mixture down from the side of the bowl if necessary.

3 Add the yogurt, seeds and lemon juice and blend until combined. Thin with a little mineral water if too thick.

4 Put several ice cubes in the bottom of a tall glass. Fill the glass to just below the brim with the Vitality Juice, leaving enough room to decorate with a few sprigs of chopped watercress on top.

VARIATIONS
For a non-dairy version of this delicious, refreshing drink, use yogurt made from goat's milk, sheep's milk or soya. A large apple can be used instead of the pear.

Energy 287kcal/1207kJ; Protein 17.8g; Carbohydrate 39.8g, of which sugars 31.2g; Fat 7.6g, of which saturates 1.6g; Cholesterol 2mg; Calcium 394mg; Fibre 8.8g; Sodium 144mg

MUESLI SMOOTHIE

LOVE MUESLI BUT DON'T LIKE THE TEXTURE? THIS DIVINELY SMOOTH DRINK HAS ALL THE GOODNESS BUT NONE OF THE LUMPY BITS. PURÉED APRICOTS AND STEM GINGER JUST ADD TO THE FLAVOUR.

Preparation: 4 minutes; Cooking: 0 minutes

SERVES TWO

INGREDIENTS
    50g/2oz/¼ cup ready-to-eat
    dried apricots
    1 piece preserved stem ginger,
    plus 30ml/2 tbsp syrup from the
    ginger jar
    40g/1½oz/scant ½ cup natural
    muesli (granola)
    about 200ml/7fl oz/scant 1 cup
    semi-skimmed (low-fat) milk

COOK'S TIP
Apricot and ginger are perfect partners in this divine drink. It makes an incredibly healthy, tasty breakfast, but is so delicious and indulgent that you could even serve it as a dessert after a summer meal. If serving it as a dessert, partner it with poached apricots.

1 Using a sharp knife, chop the dried apricots into slices or chunks. Chop the preserved ginger.

2 Put the apricots and ginger in a blender or food processor and add the syrup from the ginger jar with the muesli and milk.

3 Process until smooth, adding more milk if necessary, to make a creamy drink. Serve in wide glasses.

Energy 204kcal/865kJ; Protein 6.6g; Carbohydrate 39.1g, of which sugars 28.8g; Fat 3.4g, of which saturates 1.4g; Cholesterol 6mg; Calcium 150mg; Fibre 3.1g; Sodium 97mg

BREAKFAST <u>IN A</u> GLASS

THIS ENERGIZING BLEND IS SIMPLY BURSTING WITH GOODNESS — JUST WHAT YOU NEED WHEN YOU WAKE UP WISHING YOU COULD STAY IN YOUR COMFY BED FOR JUST AN HOUR OR SO LONGER.

Preparation: 5 minutes; Cooking: 0 minutes

SERVES TWO

INGREDIENTS
  250g/9oz firm tofu
  200g/7oz/1¾ cups strawberries
  45ml/3 tbsp pumpkin or
    sunflower seeds, plus extra
    for sprinkling
  30–45ml/2–3 tbsp clear honey
  juice of 2 large oranges
  juice of 1 lemon

VARIATION
Almost any other fruit can be used instead of the strawberries. Those with textures that blend well, such as mangoes, bananas, peaches, plums and raspberries, work particularly well as single variety substitutes, or you could try a mixture according to your taste. The juicy sweetness of mangoes and slightly tart tang of raspberries are a winning combination.

1 Roughly chop the tofu, then hull and roughly chop the strawberries. Reserve a few strawberry chunks.

2 Put all the ingredients in a blender or food processor and blend until completely smooth, scraping the mixture down from the side of the bowl, if necessary.

3 Pour into tumblers and sprinkle with extra seeds and strawberry chunks.

Energy 259kcal/1087kJ; Protein 13.3g; Carbohydrate 30.4g, of which sugars 28.2g; Fat 10.2g, of which saturates 1.1g; Cholesterol 0mg; Calcium 671mg; Fibre 1.8g; Sodium 19mg

ZINGY PAPAYA FRUIT SALAD

THIS REFRESHING, FRUITY SALAD MAKES A LOVELY LIGHT BREAKFAST, PERFECT FOR THE SUMMER MONTHS. CHOOSE REALLY RIPE, FRAGRANT PAPAYAS AND JUICY LIMES FOR THE BEST FLAVOUR.

Preparation: 5 minutes; Cooking: 0 minutes

SERVES FOUR

INGREDIENTS
2 large ripe papayas
juice of 1 fresh lime
2 pieces preserved stem ginger,
   finely sliced

VARIATION
This fruit salad is delicious made with other tropical fruit. Try using passion fruit pulp instead of the ginger, or substitute two ripe, peeled and stoned (pitted) mangoes for the papaya.

1 Cut the papayas in half lengthways. Scoop out the seeds, using a teaspoon. With a sharp knife, cut the flesh into neat, thin slices.

2 Arrange the papaya slices on a platter. Squeeze the lime juice over the papaya and sprinkle with the sliced stem ginger. Serve immediately.

Energy 112kcal/475kJ; Protein 1.6g; Carbohydrate 27.3g, of which sugars 27.3g; Fat 0.3g, of which saturates 0g; Cholesterol 0mg; Calcium 72mg; Fibre 6.8g; Sodium 16mg

CANTALOUPE MELON SALAD

LIGHTLY CARAMELIZED STRAWBERRIES LOOK PRETTY AND TASTE DIVINE IN THIS SIMPLEST OF SALADS.
SERVE IT WITH A GLASS OF CHAMPAGNE TO WELCOME GUESTS AT A SOPHISTICATED SUMMER BRUNCH.
Preparation: 3 minutes; Cooking: 4–5 minutes

SERVES FOUR

INGREDIENTS
115g/4oz/1 cup strawberries
15ml/1 tbsp icing (confectioners')
sugar, plus extra for dusting
½ cantaloupe melon

COOK'S TIP
When you need just a small amount of sifted icing (confectioners') sugar, use a tea strainer. Spoon the sugar into the strainer, then lightly tap the side with the spoon so that the sifted sugar drifts down evenly. Though tempting when you're in a hurry, mashing the sugar in the strainer with the spoon will not quicken the time it takes to sift through!

1 Preheat the grill (broiler) to high. Hull the strawberries and cut them in half. Arrange the fruit in a single layer, cut side up, on a baking sheet or in an ovenproof dish and dust with the icing sugar.

2 Grill (broil) the strawberries for 4–5 minutes, or until the sugar starts to bubble and turn golden.

3 Meanwhile, scoop out the seeds from the half melon using a spoon. Using a sharp knife, remove the skin, then cut the flesh into wedges.

4 Arrange the melon wedges attractively on a serving plate and sprinkle the lightly caramelized strawberries on top. Dust the salad with icing sugar and serve immediately.

Energy 34kcal/144kJ; Protein 0.7g; Carbohydrate 8g, of which sugars 8g; Fat 0.1g, of which saturates 0g; Cholesterol 0mg; Calcium 21mg; Fibre 1.1g; Sodium 8mg

CASHEW NUT SHAKE

THIS NUTRITIOUS DRINK TASTES SO CREAMY IT'S HARD TO BELIEVE THERE'S NOT A DROP OF MILK IN IT.
CASHEW NUTS PROVIDE THE TASTE AND TEXTURE. CHILL IT BEFORE SERVING WITH PLENTY OF ICE.

Preparation: 5 minutes; Cooking: 0 minutes

1 Finely grind the cashew nuts in a food processor. Add the sugar and cinnamon and grind the mixture again to make a smooth nut paste.

2 With the motor still running, gradually pour in 900ml/1½ pints/3¾ cups boiling water, until the drink becomes smooth and frothy. Scrape down the mixture occasionally, if necessary.

3 Pour the cashew nut milk into a jug (pitcher). Cover and chill. Stir well before serving in tall glasses, each with a couple of ice cubes on the bottom.

SERVES FOUR TO SIX

INGREDIENTS
 400g/14oz/3½ cups blanched
  cashew nuts
 225g/8oz/generous 1 cup caster
  (superfine) sugar
 1.5ml/¼ tsp ground cinnamon

COOK'S TIP
For a smooth drink, make this the night before, allow it to stand in the refrigerator overnight, and strain before serving. If the mixture seems too thick, stir in a little water but remember that the ice will dilute it as it melts, giving it a lighter texture.

Energy 555kcal/2319kJ; Protein 13.9g; Carbohydrate 51.7g, of which sugars 42.9g; Fat 33.9g, of which saturates 6.7g; Cholesterol 0mg; Calcium 43mg; Fibre 2.1g; Sodium 196mg

CRANACHAN CRUNCH

THIS TASTY BREAKFAST DISH IS BASED ON A TRADITIONAL SCOTTISH RECIPE. THE TOASTED CEREAL TASTES DELICIOUS WITH YOGURT AND A GENEROUS DRIZZLE OF HEATHER HONEY.

Preparation: 2 minutes; Cooking: 3–4 minutes

SERVES FOUR

INGREDIENTS
    75g/3oz crunchy oat cereal
    600ml/1 pint/2½ cups Greek
    (US strained plain) yogurt
    250g/9oz/1½ cups raspberries

1 Preheat the grill (broiler) to high. Spread the oat cereal on a baking sheet and place under the hot grill for 3–4 minutes until lightly toasted, stirring regularly. Set aside to cool.

2 When the oat cereal has cooled completely, fold it into the Greek yogurt, then gently fold in 200g/7oz/generous 1 cup of the raspberries, being careful not to crush the berries too much.

3 Spoon the yogurt mixture into four serving glasses or dishes, top with the remaining raspberries and serve immediately.

Energy 222kcal/935kJ; Protein 10.1g; Carbohydrate 23g, of which sugars 13.3g; Fat 10.7g, of which saturates 6.7g; Cholesterol 21mg; Calcium 250mg; Fibre 3g; Sodium 236mg

CINNAMON TOAST

THIS IS AN OLD-FASHIONED SNACK THAT IS WARMING AND COMFORTING ON A COLD DAY. CINNAMON TOAST IS PERFECT WITH A SPICY HOT CHOCOLATE DRINK OR WITH A FEW SLICES OF FRESH FRUIT.

Preparation: 2 minutes; Cooking: 2–3 minutes

SERVES TWO

INGREDIENTS

   75g/3oz/6 tbsp butter, softened
   10ml/2 tsp ground cinnamon
   30ml/2 tbsp caster (superfine) sugar,
     plus extra to serve
   4 slices bread
   prepared fresh fruit, such as
     peaches, plums, nectarines or
     mango (optional)

1 Place the softened butter in a bowl. Beat with a spoon until soft and creamy, then mix in the ground cinnamon and most of the sugar.

2 Toast the bread on both sides. Spread with the butter and sprinkle with a little remaining sugar. Serve at once, with pieces of fresh fruit, if you like.

COOK'S TIP
To round off this winter warmer, serve a quick cardamom hot chocolate with the cinnamon toast. Put 900ml/1½ pints/ 3¾ cups milk in a pan with two bruised cardamom pods and bring to the boil. Add 200g/7oz plain (semisweet) chocolate and whisk until melted. Using a slotted spoon, remove the cardamom pods just before serving.

Energy 461kcal/1921kJ; Protein 4.7g; Carbohydrate 41.6g, of which sugars 17.3g; Fat 31.8g, of which saturates 19.6g; Cholesterol 80mg; Calcium 72mg; Fibre 0.8g; Sodium 499mg

GRIDDLED TOMATOES ON SODA BREAD

NOTHING COULD BE SIMPLER THAN THIS BASIC DISH, TRANSFORMED INTO SOMETHING SPECIAL BY ADDING A DRIZZLE OF OLIVE OIL, BALSAMIC VINEGAR AND SHAVINGS OF PARMESAN CHEESE.

Preparation: 2 minutes; Cooking: 4–6 minutes

SERVES FOUR

INGREDIENTS
olive oil, for brushing and drizzling
6 tomatoes, thickly sliced
4 thick slices soda bread
balsamic vinegar, for drizzling
salt and ground black pepper
shavings of Parmesan cheese,
  to serve

COOK'S TIP
Using a griddle pan reduces the amount of oil required for cooking the tomatoes and gives them a barbecued flavour. The ridges on the pan brand the tomatoes, which look very attractive.

1 Brush a griddle pan with olive oil and heat. Add the tomato slices and cook for 4–6 minutes, turning once, until softened and slightly blackened. Alternatively, heat a grill (broiler) to high and line the rack with foil. Grill (broil) the tomato slices for 4–6 minutes, turning once, until softened.

2 While the tomatoes are cooking, lightly toast the soda bread. Place the tomatoes on top of the toast and drizzle each portion with a little olive oil and vinegar. Season to taste and serve immediately with thin shavings of Parmesan.

Energy 178kcal/751kJ; Protein 4.2g; Carbohydrate 26.3g, of which sugars 6.9g; Fat 7g, of which saturates 1g; Cholesterol 0mg; Calcium 66mg; Fibre 2.7g; Sodium 175mg

CROQUE MONSIEUR

THIS CLASSIC FRENCH TOASTIE IS DELICIOUS SERVED AT ANY TIME OF DAY, BUT WITH A FOAMING CUP OF MILKY COFFEE IT MAKES A PARTICULARLY ENJOYABLE BRUNCH DISH.

Preparation: 5 minutes; Cooking: 5 minutes

SERVES FOUR

INGREDIENTS
   8 slices white bread
   softened butter
   4 large lean ham slices
   175g/6oz Gruyère or
     mild Cheddar cheese
   ground black pepper

1 Preheat the grill (broiler) to the highest setting. Arrange the bread on the grill rack and toast four slices on both sides and the other four slices on one side only.

2 Slice the cheese thinly. Butter the slices of bread that have been toasted on both sides and top with the ham, then the cheese. Season with plenty of ground black pepper. Transfer the topped bread slices to the grill pan.

3 Lay the remaining, half-toasted bread slices on top of the cheese, with the untoasted side uppermost. Grill (broil) the tops of the sandwiches until golden brown, then cut them in half using a sharp knife and serve.

Energy 336kcal/1409kJ; Protein 20.3g; Carbohydrate 26.9g, of which sugars 1.7g; Fat 16.2g, of which saturates 9.8g; Cholesterol 57mg; Calcium 385mg; Fibre 0.8g; Sodium 897mg.

EGGS BENEDICT

USING A GOOD-QUALITY BOUGHT HOLLANDAISE FOR THIS RECIPE SAVES TIME AND MAKES ALL THE DIFFERENCE TO THE RESULT. EGGS BENEDICT ARE DELICIOUS SERVED ON TOASTED ENGLISH MUFFINS.

Preparation: 2–3 minutes; Cooking: 4–6 minutes

SERVES FOUR

INGREDIENTS
   4 large (US extra large) eggs
   4 lean ham slices
   60ml/4 tbsp warm hollandaise sauce
   2 English muffins, split
   salt and ground black pepper

COOK'S TIP
Many people complain that it's near impossible to poach a perfectly round egg – too often the edges of the cooked whites look a bit ragged. You can try swirling the simmering water with a spoon just before adding the eggs – the little currents of water help to cement the shape of the whites. Failing this, simply use a sharp knife point to trim around the edges just before serving.

1 Pour cold water into a medium pan to a depth of about 5cm/2in and bring to a gentle simmer. Crack an egg into a saucer. Swirl the water in the pan with a spoon, then slide the egg carefully into the centre of the swirl.

2 Add the second egg to the pan. Simmer both eggs for 2–3 minutes, until the whites are set, but the yolks are still soft.

3 Meanwhile, toast the muffin halves. Place on four serving plates and arrange the ham slices on top. Remove the eggs from the pan using a slotted spoon and place on top of the ham on two of the plates. Poach two more eggs and top the remaining muffins.

4 Spoon the hollandaise sauce over the eggs, season and serve immediately.

Energy 276kcal/1154kJ; Protein 14.9g; Carbohydrate 15.9g, of which sugars 1.6g; Fat 17.7g, of which saturates 3.7g; Cholesterol 258mg; Calcium 81mg; Fibre 0.7g; Sodium 520mg

PANETTONE FRENCH TOAST

THICKLY SLICED STALE WHITE BREAD IS USUALLY USED FOR FRENCH TOAST, BUT THE SLIGHTLY DRY TEXTURE OF PANETTONE MAKES A GREAT ALTERNATIVE. SERVE WITH FRESH SUMMER BERRIES.

Preparation: 2 minutes; Cooking: 4–6 minutes

SERVES FOUR

INGREDIENTS
2 large (US extra large) eggs
50g/2oz/¼ cup butter or 30ml/2 tbsp sunflower oil
4 large slices panettone, halved
30ml/2 tbsp caster (superfine) sugar
fresh berries, to serve

COOK'S TIP
A generous portion of chilled mixed berry fruits such as raspberries, blackberries, morello cherries and blueberries perfectly complements the richness of this snack.

1 Break the eggs into a bowl and whisk lightly, then tip them into a shallow dish. Heat the butter or oil in a large non-stick frying pan.

2 Dip the panettone slices in the egg and fry for 2–3 minutes on each side, until golden brown. Drain, dust with sugar and serve with the berries.

Energy 369kcal/1550kJ; Protein 9.2g; Carbohydrate 47.4g, of which sugars 19.9g; Fat 17.3g, of which saturates 8.7g; Cholesterol 123mg; Calcium 103mg; Fibre 1.7g; Sodium 349mg

KIDNEY AND MUSHROOM TOASTS

MELTINGLY TENDER LAMB'S KIDNEYS ARE A TRADITIONAL BREAKFAST TREAT. COOKING THEM WITH MUSHROOMS IN MUSTARD BUTTER FLATTERS THEIR FLAVOUR, AND THEY TASTE GREAT ON TOAST.

Preparation: 5 minutes; Cooking: 4–6 minutes

SERVES TWO TO FOUR

INGREDIENTS
- 4 large, flat field (portabello) mushrooms, stalks trimmed
- 75g/3oz/6 tbsp butter, softened
- 10ml/2 tsp wholegrain mustard
- 15ml/1 tbsp chopped fresh parsley
- 4 lamb's kidneys, skinned, halved and cored
- 4 thick slices of brown bread, cut into rounds and toasted
- sprig of parsley, to garnish
- tomato wedges, to serve

COOK'S TIPS
• Kidneys are best served when they are still pink in the centre.
• Serve the mixture on halved, warm scones, if you prefer.

1 Wash the mushrooms, pat dry with kitchen paper and remove the stalks.

2 Mix the butter, wholegrain mustard and fresh parsley together.

3 Rinse the prepared lamb's kidneys well under cold running water, and pat dry with kitchen paper.

4 Melt about two-thirds of the butter mixture in a large frying pan and fry the mushrooms and kidneys for 2–3 minutes on each side.

5 When the kidneys are cooked to your liking spread with the remaining herb butter. Pile on the hot toast and serve with the tomato, garnished with parsley.

Energy 379kcal/1580kJ; Protein 20.1g; Carbohydrate 14.9g, of which sugars 1g; Fat 27.1g, of which saturates 15.9g; Cholesterol 353mg; Calcium 59mg; Fibre 1.7g; Sodium 560mg

WARM PANCAKES WITH CARAMELIZED PEARS

IF YOU CAN FIND THEM, USE WILLIAMS PEARS FOR THIS RECIPE BECAUSE THEY ARE SO JUICY. FOR A REALLY INDULGENT BREAKFAST, TOP WITH A SPOONFUL OF CRÈME FRAICHE OR FROMAGE FRAIS.

Preparation: 5 minutes; Cooking: 6 minutes

SERVES FOUR

INGREDIENTS

8 ready-made pancakes
50g/2oz/¼ cup butter
4 ripe pears, peeled, cored and
   thickly sliced
30ml/2 tbsp light muscovado
   (brown) sugar
crème fraîche or fromage frais,
   to serve

1 Preheat the oven to 150°C/300°F/ Gas 2. Tightly wrap the pancakes in foil and place in the oven to warm through.

VARIATION
This tastes just as good with sliced nectarines instead of pears.

2 Meanwhile, heat the butter in a large frying pan and add the pears. Fry for 2–3 minutes, until the undersides are golden. Turn the pears over and sprinkle with sugar. Cook for a further 2–3 minutes, or until the sugar dissolves and the pan juices become sticky.

3 Remove the pancakes from the oven and take them out of the foil. Divide the pears among them, placing them in one quarter. Fold each pancake in half over the filling, then into quarters and place two folded pancakes on each plate. Drizzle the pan juices over and serve with crème fraîche or fromage frais.

Energy 544kcal/2274kJ; Protein 7.7g; Carbohydrate 64.9g, of which sugars 42.4g; Fat 29.9g, of which saturates 6.5g; Cholesterol 27mg; Calcium 155mg; Fibre 4.3g; Sodium 144mg

OATMEAL PANCAKES WITH BACON

WRAP AN OATMEAL PANCAKE AROUND A CRISP SLICE OF BEST BACON AND SAMPLE A NEW TASTE SENSATION WITH YOUR TRADITIONAL COOKED BREAKFAST. IT MAKES A GREAT EGG DIPPER, TOO.

Preparation: 2–3 minutes; Cooking: 12 minutes

MAKES FOUR PANCAKES

INGREDIENTS
  50g/2oz/½ cup fine wholemeal
    (whole-wheat) flour
  30ml/2 tbsp fine pinhead oatmeal
  pinch of salt
  1 egg
  about 150ml/¼ pint/⅔ cup
    buttermilk or milk
  butter or oil, for greasing
  4 rashers (strips) bacon

COOK'S TIP
The oatmeal in the batter gives it texture, so these pancakes are firmer than conventional crêpes. You can easily double or treble the mixture and even make it ahead of time. It will thicken on standing, though, so thin it with buttermilk or milk before use.

1 Mix the flour, oatmeal and salt in a bowl, beat in the egg and add enough buttermilk or milk to make a creamy batter of the same consistency as that used for ordinary pancakes.

2 Thoroughly heat a griddle or cast-iron frying pan over a medium-hot heat. When very hot, grease the surface lightly with butter or oil.

3 Pour in the batter, about a ladleful at a time. Tilt the frying pan to spread evenly and cook the pancake for about 2 minutes until set and the underside is browned. Turn over and cook for 1 minute until browned.

4 Keep the pancake warm while you cook the others and fry the bacon. Roll the pancakes around the bacon to serve.

Energy 148kcal/621kJ; Protein 9.7g; Carbohydrate 13.1g, of which sugars 2g; Fat 6.7g, of which saturates 2.2g; Cholesterol 64mg; Calcium 62mg; Fibre 1.5g; Sodium 469mg

SWEET BREAKFAST OMELETTE

FOR A HEARTY START TO A DAY WHEN YOU KNOW YOU'RE GOING TO BE TOO RUSHED TO HAVE MUCH MORE THAN AN APPLE FOR LUNCH, TRY THIS SWEET OMELETTE WITH A SPOONFUL OF JAM.

Preparation: 3 minutes; Cooking: 5 minutes

SERVES ONE

INGREDIENTS
   3 eggs
   10ml/2 tsp caster (superfine) sugar
   5ml/1 tsp plain (all-purpose) flour
   10g/¼oz/½ tbsp unsalted
     (sweet) butter
   bread and jam, to serve

COOK'S TIP
Although this recipe is stated to serve one, it is substantial enough for two not-very-hungry people. Omelettes are best eaten the moment they emerge from the pan, so if you are cooking for a crowd, get each to make their own and eat in relays.

1 Break the eggs into a large bowl, add the sugar and flour and beat until really frothy. Heat the butter in an omelette pan until it begins to bubble, then pour in the egg mixture and cook, without stirring, until it begins to set.

2 Run a wooden spatula around the edge of the omelette, then carefully turn it over and cook the second side for 1–2 minutes until golden. Serve hot or warm with thick slices of fresh bread and a bowlful of fruity jam.

Energy 351kcal/1465kJ; Protein 19.3g; Carbohydrate 14.4g, of which sugars 10.6g; Fat 24.9g, of which saturates 9.9g; Cholesterol 592mg; Calcium 100mg; Fibre 0.2g; Sodium 271mg

CHIVE SCRAMBLED EGGS IN BRIOCHES

THESE CREAMY SCRAMBLED EGGS ARE DELICIOUS AT ANY TIME OF DAY BUT, WHEN SERVED WITH
FRANCE'S FAVOURITE BREAKFAST BREAD, THEY BECOME THE ULTIMATE BREAKFAST OR BRUNCH TREAT.

Preparation: 6 minutes; Cooking: 7 minutes

SERVES FOUR

INGREDIENTS
 4 individual brioches
 6 eggs, beaten
 45ml/3 tbsp chopped fresh chives,
  plus extra to serve
 25g/1oz/2 tbsp butter
 45ml/3 tbsp cottage cheese
 60–75ml/4–5 tbsp double
  (heavy) cream
 salt and ground black pepper

1 Preheat the oven to 180°C/350°F/
Gas 4. Cut the tops off the brioches and
set to one side. Carefully scoop out the
centre of each brioche, leaving a bread
case. Put the brioche cases and lids on
a baking sheet and bake for 5 minutes
until hot and crisp.

2 Meanwhile, beat the eggs lightly and
season to taste. Add about one-third of
the chopped chives. Heat the butter in a
medium pan until it begins to foam, then
add the eggs and cook, stirring constantly
with a wooden spoon until semi-solid.

3 Stir in the cottage cheese, cream and
half the remaining chives. Cook for
1–2 minutes more, making sure that the
eggs remain soft and creamy.

COOK'S TIP
Save the scooped-out brioche centres
and freeze them in an airtight container.
Partly defrost and blend or grate them
to make crumbs for coating fish or
pieces of chicken before frying.

4 To serve, spoon the eggs into the
crisp brioche shells and sprinkle with
the remaining chives.

VARIATION
If you do not happen to have brioches to
hand, these wonderful herby eggs taste
delicious on top of thick slices of toasted
bread. Try them piled high on warm
focaccia, or on toasted ciabatta, Granary
(whole-wheat) bread or muffins.

Energy 414kcal/1731kJ; Protein 16.2g; Carbohydrate 32.5g, of which sugars 10.5g; Fat 25.5g, of which saturates 12g; Cholesterol 322mg; Calcium 154mg; Fibre 1.9g; Sodium 374mg

SCRAMBLED EGGS WITH ANCHOVIES

LIFTING THE SPIRITS ON THE DULLEST OF DAYS SCRAMBLED EGGS ARE TRUE COMFORT FOOD.
THIS VERSION COMBINES WITH ANCHOVIES, WHOSE SALTY TANG IS SUPERB WITH THE CREAMY EGG.

Preparation: 2–3 minutes; Cooking: 7 minutes

SERVES TWO

INGREDIENTS

2 slices bread
40g/1½oz/3 tbsp butter, plus
   extra for spreading
anchovy paste, such as
   Gentleman's Relish, for spreading
2 eggs and 2 egg yolks, beaten
60–90ml/4–6 tbsp single (light)
   cream or milk
ground black pepper
anchovy fillets, cut into strips,
   and paprika, to garnish

COOK'S TIP

These creamy scrambled eggs are
delicious in baked potatoes instead of
on toast. Serve with a salad and a glass
of crisp white wine for a tasty lunch.

1 Toast the bread, spread with butter
and anchovy paste, then remove the
crusts and cut into triangles. Keep warm.

2 Melt the rest of the butter in a
medium non-stick pan, then stir in the
beaten eggs, cream or milk, and a little
ground pepper. Heat very gently, stirring
constantly, until the mixture begins
to thicken.

3 Remove the pan from the heat and
continue to stir until the mixture
becomes very creamy, but do not allow
it to harden.

4 Divide the scrambled eggs among the
triangles of toast and garnish each one
with strips of anchovy fillet and a
generous sprinkling of paprika. Serve
immediately, while still hot.

Energy 405kcal/1680kJ; Protein 12.6g; Carbohydrate 14.1g, of which sugars 1.5g; Fat 33.7g, of which saturates 17.2g; Cholesterol 451mg; Calcium 112mg; Fibre 0.4g; Sodium 350mg

LOX WITH BAGELS AND CREAM CHEESE

THIS SOPHISTICATED DISH IS PERFECT FOR A WEEKEND BREAKFAST OR BRUNCH WITH FRIENDS. LOX IS THE JEWISH WORD FOR SMOKED SALMON, AND THIS DELI CLASSIC IS EASY TO MAKE AT HOME.

Preparation: 3 minutes; Cooking: 4–5 minutes

SERVES 2

INGREDIENTS
  2 bagels
  115–175g/4–6oz/½–¾ cup full-fat
    cream cheese
  150g/5oz sliced best smoked salmon
  ground black pepper
  lemon wedges, to serve

1 Preheat the oven to 200°C/400°F/ Gas 6. Put the bagels on a large baking sheet and warm them in the oven for 4–5 minutes.

2 Remove the bagels from the oven, split them in two and spread each half generously with cream cheese. Pile the salmon on top of the bagel bases and grind over plenty of black pepper.

3 Squeeze over some lemon juice, then add the bagel tops, at an angle.

4 Place on serving plates with the lemon wedges. If you have time, wrap each lemon wedge in a small square of muslin (cheesecloth), tie with fine string and put it on the plate.

COOK'S TIP
It is essential to be generous with the smoked salmon and to use the best cream cheese you can find – absolutely not a low-fat version.

Energy 496kcal/2068kJ; Protein 25.9g; Carbohydrate 28.9g, of which sugars 3.3g; Fat 31.6g, of which saturates 17.7g; Cholesterol 81mg; Calcium 71mg; Fibre 1.2g; Sodium 1858mg

LIGHT BITES AND APPETIZERS

Sitting down to a leisurely meal is a luxury few of us allow ourselves these days. We read longingly about Mediterranean meals that start at 2 and end at 5, with the whole family sitting around a scrubbed wooden table in the garden, but the reality for most of us is that there are appointments to be kept and jobs to be finished. However, a fast-paced weekday routine need not mean running on empty until we can finally sit down to an evening meal. This chapter is packed with easy, tasty dishes, some of which will make excellent lunchtime options. A simple meal of Butterbean and Sun-dried Tomato Soup followed by Walnut and Goat's Cheese Bruschetta is hard to beat — and perfect for those occasions where friends stop by for a quick bite to eat. If you prefer something hot to kick-start the afternoon, there is Smoked Salmon and Chive Omelette or Warm Dressed Salad with Poached Egg, or Jugged Kippers — surely the ultimate, healthy "fast food" and as sumptuous when served as a mid-afternoon snack as for a super-fast, nutritious supper prior to dashing out.

AVOCADO SOUP

THIS DELICIOUS SOUP HAS A FRESH, DELICATE FLAVOUR AND A WONDERFUL COLOUR. FOR ADDED ZEST, ADD A GENEROUS SQUEEZE OF LIME OR LEMON JUICE JUST BEFORE SERVING.

Preparation: 3 minutes; Cooking: 3–4 minutes

SERVES FOUR

INGREDIENTS

2 large ripe avocados
300ml/½ pint/1¼ cups sour cream
1 litre/1¾ pints/4 cups
  well-flavoured chicken stock
a small bunch of fresh coriander
  (cilantro), chopped
salt and ground black pepper

COOK'S TIP
Choose ripe avocados for this soup – they should feel soft when gently pressed. Keep very firm avocados at room temperature for 3–4 days until they soften. To speed ripening, place in a brown paper bag.

1 Cut the avocados in half, remove the peel and lift out the stones (pits). Chop the flesh coarsely and place it in a food processor with 45–60ml/3–4 tbsp of the sour cream. Process until smooth.

2 Heat the chicken stock in a pan. When it is hot, but still below simmering point, add the rest of the sour cream and stir gently to mix.

3 Gradually stir the avocado mixture into the hot stock. Heat gently but do not let the mixture approach boiling point. Add salt to taste.

4 Ladle the soup into heated bowls and sprinkle each portion with chopped coriander and black pepper. Serve immediately, as it will discolour on standing.

Energy 343kcal/1416kJ; Protein 4.4g; Carbohydrate 5.1g, of which sugars 3.6g; Fat 33.9g, of which saturates 13.4g; Cholesterol 45mg; Calcium 106mg; Fibre 4g; Sodium 41mg

BUTTER BEAN AND SUN-DRIED TOMATO SOUP

THIS SOUP IS QUICK AND EASY TO MAKE. THE KEY IS TO USE A GOOD QUALITY HOME-MADE OR BOUGHT FRESH STOCK WITH PLENTY OF PESTO AND SUN-DRIED TOMATO PURÉE.

Preparation: 2 minutes; Cooking: 12 minutes

SERVES FOUR

INGREDIENTS
  2 x 400g/14oz cans butter (lima)
    beans, drained and rinsed
  900ml/1½ pints/3¾ cups chicken
    or vegetable stock
  60ml/4 tbsp sun-dried tomato
    purée (paste)
  75ml/5 tbsp pesto

COOK'S TIP
For the busy cook, good-quality bought stocks are a blessing. Most large supermarkets now sell fresh stock in tubs. Another good product is concentrated liquid stock, sold in bottles. However, if you cannot find any of the above, a good-quality stock cube will do the job.

1 Put the butter beans in a pan. Stir in the stock and bring to the boil over a medium heat, stirring once or twice.

2 Stir in the tomato purée and pesto. Lower the heat and cook gently for 5 minutes.

3 Transfer six ladlefuls of the soup to a blender or food processor, scooping up plenty of the beans. Process until smooth, then return the purée to the pan.

4 Heat gently, stirring frequently, for 5 minutes, then season if necessary. Ladle into four warmed soup bowls and serve with warm crusty bread or breadsticks.

Energy 269kcal/1130kJ; Protein 15.6g; Carbohydrate 28.3g, of which sugars 4.5g; Fat 11.2g, of which saturates 2.5g; Cholesterol 6mg; Calcium 111mg; Fibre 9.7g; Sodium 944mg

ARTICHOKE AND CUMIN DIP

THIS DIP IS SO EASY TO MAKE AND IS UNBELIEVABLY TASTY. SERVE WITH OLIVES, HUMMUS AND WEDGES OF PITTA BREAD AS AN INFORMAL SUMMERY SNACK SELECTION.

Preparation: 2 minutes; Cooking: 0 minutes

SERVES FOUR

INGREDIENTS

2 x 400g/14oz cans artichoke
   hearts, drained
2 garlic cloves, peeled
2.5ml/½ tsp ground cumin
olive oil
salt and ground black pepper

VARIATIONS

Grilled (broiled) artichokes bottled in oil have a fabulous flavour and can be used instead of canned artichokes. Try adding a handful of basil leaves to the artichokes before blending.

1 Put the artichoke hearts in a food processor with the garlic and ground cumin, and add a generous drizzle of olive oil. Process to a smooth purée and season with plenty of salt and ground black pepper to taste.

2 Spoon the purée into a serving bowl and serve with an extra drizzle of olive oil swirled on the top and slices of warm pitta bread or wholemeal (whole-wheat) toast fingers and carrot sticks for dipping.

Energy 76kcal/315kJ; Protein 1.6g; Carbohydrate 3.9g, of which sugars 3.5g; Fat 6.2g, of which saturates 1g; Cholesterol 0mg; Calcium 18mg; Fibre 3.5g; Sodium 4mg

CHICKEN LIVER <u>AND</u> BRANDY PATÉ

THIS PATÉ REALLY COULD NOT BE SIMPLER TO PUT TOGETHER, AND TASTES SO MUCH BETTER THAN ANYTHING YOU CAN BUY READY-MADE IN THE SUPERMARKETS. SERVE WITH CRISPY MELBA TOAST.

Preparation: 3 minutes; Cooking: 5–6 minutes; Make ahead

SERVES FOUR

INGREDIENTS

50g/2oz/¼ cup butter
350g/12oz chicken livers, trimmed
   and roughly chopped
30ml/2 tbsp brandy
30ml/2 tbsp double (heavy) cream
salt and ground black pepper

1 Heat the butter in a large frying pan. Add the chicken livers. Cook over a medium heat for 3–4 minutes, or until browned and cooked through.

2 Add the brandy and allow to bubble for a few minutes. Let the mixture cool slightly, then place in a food processor with the cream and some salt and pepper.

3 Process the mixture until smooth and spoon into ramekin dishes. Level the surface and chill overnight to set. If making more than 1 day ahead, seal the surface of each portion with a layer of melted butter. Serve garnished with sprigs of parsley to add a little colour.

Energy 227kcal/942kJ; Protein 15.7g; Carbohydrate 0.2g, of which sugars 0.2g; Fat 16.3g, of which saturates 9.6g; Cholesterol 369mg; Calcium 13mg; Fibre 0g; Sodium 144mg

WALNUT AND GOAT'S CHEESE BRUSCHETTA

THE COMBINATION OF TOASTED WALNUTS AND MELTING GOAT'S CHEESE IS LOVELY IN THIS SIMPLE LUNCHTIME SNACK, WHICH CAN BE SERVED WITH A DRESSED SALAD IF THE OCCASION CALLS FOR IT.

Preparation: 5 minutes; Cooking: 3–5 minutes

SERVES FOUR

INGREDIENTS

    50g/2oz/½ cup walnut pieces
    4 thick slices walnut bread
    120ml/4fl oz/½ cup French dressing
    200g/7oz chèvre or other semi-soft
      goat's cheese

COOK'S TIP
Walnut bread is sold in most large supermarkets and makes an interesting alternative to ordinary crusty bread, although a freshly baked loaf of the latter is fine if speciality breads are not available. If using crusty bread, try to find a slender loaf to slice, so that the portions are not too wide. If you can only buy a large loaf, cut the slices in half to make neat, chunky pieces.

1 Preheat the grill (broiler). Spread out the walnut pieces on a baking sheet. Lightly toast them, shivering the baking sheet once or twice so that they cook evenly, then remove and set aside.

2 Put the walnut bread on a foil-lined grill rack and toast on one side. Turn the slices over and drizzle each with 15ml/1 tbsp of the dressing.

3 Cut the goat's cheese into twelve slices and place three on each piece of bread. Grill (broil) for about 3 minutes, until the cheese is melting and beginning to brown.

4 Transfer the bruschetta to serving plates, sprinkle with the toasted walnuts and drizzle with the remaining French dressing. Serve the bruschetta immediately with salad leaves.

Energy 558kcal/2321kJ; Protein 16.7g; Carbohydrate 25.6g, of which sugars 2.2g; Fat 37.2g, of which saturates 12.7g; Cholesterol 47mg; Calcium 137mg; Fibre 1.2g; Sodium 841mg

MUSHROOMS ON SPICY TOAST

DRY-PANNING IS A QUICK WAY OF COOKING MUSHROOMS THAT MAKES THE MOST OF THEIR FLAVOUR.
THE JUICES RUN WHEN THE MUSHROOMS ARE HEATED, SO THEY BECOME REALLY MOIST AND TENDER.

Preparation: 2–3 minutes; Cooking: 4–5 minutes

SERVES FOUR

INGREDIENTS

8–12 large flat field (portabello)
  mushrooms
50g/1oz/2 tbsp butter
5ml/1 tsp curry paste
salt
4 slices thickly-sliced white bread,
  toasted, to serve

1 Preheat the oven to 200°C/400°F/
Gas 6. Peel the mushrooms, if
necessary, and remove the stalks. Heat
a dry frying pan until very hot.

2 Place the mushrooms in the hot frying
pan, with the gills on top. Using half
the butter, add a piece the size of a
hazelnut to each one, then sprinkle all
the mushrooms lightly with salt.

3 Cook over a medium heat until the
butter begins to bubble and the
mushrooms are juicy and tender.

4 Meanwhile, mix the remaining butter
with the curry powder. Spread on the
bread. Bake in the oven for 10 minutes,
pile the mushrooms on top and serve.

VARIATIONS
• Using a flavoured butter makes these
mushrooms even more special. Try one of
the following:
• **Herb butter** Mix softened butter with
chopped fresh herbs such as parsley and
thyme, or marjoram and chopped chives.
• **Olive butter** Mix softened butter with diced
green olives and spring onions (scallions).
• **Tomato butter** Mix softened butter with
sun-dried tomato purée (paste).
• **Garlic butter** Mix softened butter with
finely chopped garlic.
• **Pepper and Paprika butter** Mix softened
butter with 2.5ml/½ tsp paprika and
2.5ml/½ tsp black pepper.

Energy 230kcal/966kJ; Protein 6.1g; Carbohydrate 25.1g, of which sugars 1.6g; Fat 12.5g, of which saturates 6.7g; Cholesterol 27mg; Calcium 63mg; Fibre 1.9g; Sodium 341mg

GOLDEN GRUYÈRE AND BASIL TORTILLAS

TORTILLA FLIP-OVERS ARE A GREAT INVENTION. ONCE YOU'VE TRIED THIS RECIPE, YOU'LL WANT TO EXPERIMENT WITH DIFFERENT FILLINGS AND LEFTOVERS WILL NEVER GO TO WASTE AGAIN.

Preparation: 1–2 minutes; Cooking: 4 minutes

SERVES TWO

INGREDIENTS
   15ml/1 tbsp olive oil
   2 soft flour tortillas
   115g/4oz Gruyère cheese,
     thinly sliced
   a handful of fresh basil leaves
   salt and ground black pepper

VARIATION
These crisp tortillas make excellent snacks to share with friends on a night in. If you have a few slices of ham or salami in the refrigerator, add these to the tortillas – or simply prepare a mixture of the two to satisfy a range of palates.

1 Heat the oil in a frying pan over a medium heat. Add one of the tortillas, and heat through for 1 minute.

2 Arrange the Gruyère cheese slices and basil leaves on top of the tortilla and season with salt and pepper.

3 Place the remaining tortilla on top to make a sandwich and flip the whole thing over with a metal spatula. Cook for a few minutes, until the underneath is golden.

4 Slide the tortilla sandwich on to a chopping board or plate and cut into wedges. Serve immediately.

Energy 354kcal/1474kJ; Protein 16.4g; Carbohydrate 15g, of which sugars 0.4g; Fat 24.6g, of which saturates 13.3g; Cholesterol 56mg; Calcium 453mg; Fibre 0.6g; Sodium 486mg

OMELETTE ARNOLD BENNETT

CONTRIVING TO BE CREAMY AND FLUFFY AT THE SAME TIME, THIS SMOKED HADDOCK SOUFFLÉ OMELETTE IS DELICIOUS. NO WONDER THE AUTHOR ARNOLD BENNETT LOVED IT SO MUCH.

Preparation: 2 minutes; Cooking: 12 minutes

SERVES TWO

INGREDIENTS
175g/6oz smoked haddock fillet
  (preferably undyed if available)
50g/2oz/4 tbsp butter, diced
175ml/6fl oz/¾ cup whipping or
  double (heavy) cream
4 eggs, separated
40g/1½oz/⅓ cup mature (sharp)
  Cheddar cheese, grated
ground black pepper
watercress, to garnish

1 Put the haddock in a shallow pan with water to cover and poach over a medium heat for 8–10 minutes or until the fish flakes easily when tested with the tip of a knife. Drain well.

2 Remove the skin and any bones from the haddock fillet and discard. Carefully flake the flesh using a fork.

3 Melt half the butter with 60ml/4 tbsp of the cream in a fairly small non-stick pan, then add the flaked fish and stir together gently. Cover the pan and remove from the heat. Preheat the grill (broiler).

4 Mix the egg yolks with 15ml/1 tbsp of the cream. Season with pepper, then stir into the fish. Mix the cheese and the remaining cream. Whisk the egg whites until stiff, then fold into the fish mixture. Heat the remaining butter in an omelette pan, add the fish mixture and cook until browned underneath. Pour the cheese mixture over and grill (broil) until bubbling. Garnish and serve.

Energy 821kcal/3396kJ; Protein 36.1g; Carbohydrate 2.6g, of which sugars 2.6g; Fat 74g, of which saturates 42.6g; Cholesterol 577mg; Calcium 280mg; Fibre 0g; Sodium 1123mg

SMOKED SALMON AND CHIVE OMELETTE

THE ADDITION OF A GENEROUS PORTION OF CHOPPED SMOKED SALMON GIVES A REALLY LUXURIOUS FINISH TO THIS SIMPLE, CLASSIC DISH, WHICH IS AN IDEAL QUICK LUNCH FOR TWO PEOPLE.

Preparation: 2–3 minutes; Cooking: 5–6 minutes

SERVES TWO

INGREDIENTS
4 eggs
15ml/1 tbsp chopped fresh chives or
   spring onions (scallions)
a knob (pat) of butter
50g/2oz smoked salmon,
   roughly chopped
salt and ground black pepper

1 Break the eggs into a bowl. Beat with a fork until just combined, then stir in the chopped fresh chives or spring onions. Season with salt and a generous sprinkling of freshly ground black pepper, and set aside.

2 Heat the butter in a medium frying pan until foamy. Pour in the eggs and cook over a medium heat for 3–4 minutes, drawing the cooked egg from around the edge into the centre of the pan from time to time.

3 At this stage, you can either leave the top of the omelette slightly soft or finish it off under the grill (broiler), depending on how you like your omelette. Top with the smoked salmon, fold the omelette over and cut in half to serve.

Energy 221kcal/920kJ; Protein 19g; Carbohydrate 0.2g, of which sugars 0.2g; Fat 16.4g, of which saturates 5.9g; Cholesterol 400mg; Calcium 65mg; Fibre 0.1g; Sodium 641mg

PEA AND MINT OMELETTE

SERVE THIS DELICIOUSLY LIGHT OMELETTE WITH CRUSTY BREAD AND A GREEN SALAD FOR A FRESH AND TASTY LUNCH. WHEN THEY ARE IN SEASON, USE FRESHLY SHELLED PEAS INSTEAD OF FROZEN ONES.

Preparation: 2 minutes; Cooking: 8–10 minutes

SERVES TWO

INGREDIENTS
    50g/2oz/½ cup frozen peas
    4 eggs
    30ml/2 tbsp chopped fresh mint
    a knob (pat) of butter
    salt and ground black pepper

VARIATION
When young broad (fava) beans are in season, use them instead of peas. Shell the beans and cook them in boiling salted water for 3–4 minutes until just tender. Meanwhile, grill (broil) 3–4 slices of bacon. Add the beans to the egg mixture instead of the peas and crumble the bacon over the omelette when it is almost cooked.

1 Break the eggs into a large bowl and beat with a fork. Season well with salt and pepper and set aside.

2 Cook the peas in a large pan of salted boiling water for 3–4 minutes until tender. Drain well in a colander and add to the eggs in the bowl. Stir in the chopped fresh mint and swirl with a spoon until thoroughly combined.

3 Heat the butter in a medium frying pan until foamy. Pour in the egg mixture and cook over a medium heat for 3–4 minutes, drawing in the cooked egg from the edges from time to time, until the mixture is nearly set.

4 Finish off cooking the omelette under a hot grill (broiler) until set and golden. Carefully fold the omelette over, cut it in half and serve immediately.

Energy 208kcal/865kJ; Protein 14.6g; Carbohydrate 3.3g, of which sugars 0.6g; Fat 15.7g, of which saturates 5.8g; Cholesterol 391mg; Calcium 79mg; Fibre 1.2g; Sodium 172mg

WHITEFISH SALAD <u>WITH</u> TOASTED BAGELS

A TRADITIONAL DELI FAVOURITE, SMOKED WHITEFISH MAKES A SUPERB SALAD. IF YOU CAN'T FIND IT, USE SMOKED HALIBUT, BUT DON'T PASS UP THE BAGELS, WHICH ARE THE PERFECT ACCOMPANIMENT.

Preparation: 8–10 minutes; Cooking: 0 minutes

SERVES FOUR TO SIX

INGREDIENTS

1 smoked whitefish or halibut, skinned and boned
2 celery sticks, chopped
½ red, white or yellow onion or 3–5 spring onions (scallions), chopped
45ml/3 tbsp mayonnaise
45ml/3 tbsp sour cream
juice of ½–1 lemon
1 round lettuce
ground black pepper
5–10ml/1–2 tsp chopped fresh parsley, to garnish
toasted bagels, to serve

1 Break the smoked fish into bitesize pieces. In a bowl, combine the chopped celery, onion or spring onion, mayonnaise and sour cream, and add lemon juice to taste.

2 Fold the fish into the mixture and season with pepper. Arrange the lettuce leaves on serving plates, then spoon the smoked fish salad on top. Sprinkle with parsley and serve with bagels.

Energy 108kcal/450kJ; Protein 7.8g; Carbohydrate 1.6g, of which sugars 1.3g; Fat 7.9g, of which saturates 1.9g; Cholesterol 22mg; Calcium 29mg; Fibre 0.4g; Sodium 64mg

WARM DRESSED SALAD WITH POACHED EGGS

SOFT POACHED EGGS, CHILLI, HOT CROÛTONS AND COOL, CRISP SALAD LEAVES MAKE A LIVELY AND UNUSUAL COMBINATION. THIS SIMPLE SALAD IS PERFECT AT ANY TIME OF DAY.

Preparation: 2–3 minutes; Cooking: 10–12 minutes

SERVES TWO

INGREDIENTS
½ small loaf wholemeal
  (whole-wheat) bread
45ml/3 tbsp chilli oil
2 eggs
115g/4oz mixed salad leaves
45ml/3 tbsp extra virgin olive oil
2 garlic cloves, crushed
15ml/1 tbsp balsamic or
  sherry vinegar
50g/2oz Parmesan cheese, shaved
ground black pepper

1 Carefully cut the crust from the Granary loaf and discard. Cut the bread into neat slices and then into 2.5cm/1in cubes.

2 Heat the chilli oil in a large frying pan. Add the bread cubes and cook for about 5 minutes, tossing the cubes occasionally, until they are crisp and golden brown all over.

3 Meanwhile, bring a pan of water to the boil. Break each egg into a jug and carefully slide into the water, one at a time. Gently poach the eggs for about 4 minutes until lightly cooked.

4 Divide the salad leaves between two plates. Remove the croûtons from the pan and arrange them over the leaves.

5 Wipe the pan clean with kitchen paper. Then heat the olive oil in the pan, add the garlic and vinegar and cook over high heat for 1 minute. Pour the warm dressing over the salads.

6 Place a poached egg on each salad. Top with thin Parmesan shavings and a little ground black pepper.

Energy 697kcal/2907kJ; Protein 25.9g; Carbohydrate 41.3g, of which sugars 2.8g; Fat 49g, of which saturates 11.5g; Cholesterol 215mg; Calcium 408mg; Fibre 6.3g; Sodium 914mg

BACON SALAD WITH CAMEMBERT DRESSING

FRIED APPLES AND BACON ARE PERFECT PARTNERS. HERE THEY ARE HEAPED OVER CRISP LETTUCE TO MAKE AN IRRESISTIBLE SALAD. A WARM TANGY CHEESE DRESSING ADDS THE FINISHING TOUCH.

Preparation: 5 minutes; Cooking: 4–5 minutes

SERVES FOUR

INGREDIENTS
  30ml/2 tbsp olive oil
  50g/2oz diced streaky (fatty) bacon
    slices, preferably dry-cured, diced
  1 eating apple, cored and chopped
  2 small heads cos or romaine lettuce
  a squeeze of lemon juice
  salt and ground black pepper
For the dressing
  150ml/¼ pint/⅔ cup sour cream
  15ml/1 tbsp cider
  50g/2oz Camembert or similar
    cheese, chopped
  a dash of cider vinegar

VARIATION
For a slightly tangier topping, replace the Camembert with a mild and creamy blue cheese, such as Cambozola.

1 Heat 15ml/1 tbsp of the olive oil in a large frying pan and add the diced streaky bacon. Cook over a medium heat until crisp and golden. Add the chopped apple and cook gently for 1–2 minutes until golden brown and softened.

2 Tear the cos or romain lettuce carefully into bitesize pieces.

3 To make the dressing, heat the sour cream, cider, cheese and vinegar together in a small pan over a low heat until smooth and creamy.

4 Toss the lettuce with the remaining oil and the lemon juice, season, then divide among four plates. Heap the warm apple and bacon on top, then drizzle over the dressing.

Energy 190kcal/785kJ; Protein 5.9g; Carbohydrate 3.5g, of which sugars 3.5g; Fat 16.7g, of which saturates 8.4g; Cholesterol 42mg; Calcium 76mg; Fibre 0.5g; Sodium 244mg

JUGGED KIPPERS

THE DEMAND FOR NATURALLY SMOKED KIPPERS IS EVER INCREASING. THEY ARE DELICIOUS SERVED WITH BUTTER, LEMON JUICE SQUEEZED OVER AND CRUSTY BREAD, AND ARE PREPARED IN MINUTES.

Preparation: 2–3 minutes; Cooking: 5–6 minutes

SERVES FOUR

INGREDIENTS
    4 kippers (smoked herrings),
      preferably naturally smoked,
      whole or filleted
    25g/1oz/2 tbsp butter
    ground black pepper
    lemon wedges, to serve

1 Select a heatproof glass jug (pitcher) tall enough for the kippers to be immersed when the water is added. If the heads are still on the kippers, remove them.

2 Put the fish into the jug, tails up, and then cover them with boiling water. Leave for about 5 minutes, until tender.

3 Drain well and serve on warmed plates with butter, a little black pepper and the lemon wedges.

Energy 248kcal/1025kJ; Protein 15.9g; Carbohydrate 0g, of which sugars 0g; Fat 20.4g, of which saturates 5.8g; Cholesterol 68mg; Calcium 49mg; Fibre 0g; Sodium 776mg

FISH AND MEAT DISHES

When you only have a little time to produce a first-class meal, you need to make sure your ingredients are of the finest quality. Grilled fish, topped with butter or spices, is a great choice when time is tight, but if you fancy something a little meatier, you'll need tender cuts: well hung beef steak and strips of lamb or pork fillet (tenderloin). Befriending your local butcher can be the best move you ever make: describe what you plan to cook and ask for advice. Many of these dishes are served with complementary dressings, sauces, salads and fruit — easy yet original touches to transform an everyday meal into a showpiece. Some, such as Fiery Chicken Wings with Blood Oranges, will make stylish al fresco options for the barbecue season, while others, such as the warming Lamb's Kidneys with Mustard Sauce, are perfect cold-weather comfort fare. All the recipes are quick and easy to cook, proving that fast food need not mean forgoing your favourite meats, and if you rope in a few kitchen helpers for the preparation, with the promise of a share in the spoils once cooked, they'll be ready in even less time.

GRILLED SOLE <u>WITH</u> CHIVE BUTTER

THE BEST WAY OF TRANSFORMING SIMPLE GRILLED FISH INTO A LUXURY DISH IS BY TOPPING IT WITH A FLAVOURED BUTTER. THIS ONE, FLAVOURED WITH LEMON GRASS AND LIME, IS A WINNER.

Preparation: 3–4 minutes; Cooking: 10 minutes

SERVES FOUR

INGREDIENTS
  115g/4oz/½ cup unsalted (sweet)
    butter, softened, plus extra, melted
  5ml/1 tsp diced lemon grass
  pinch of finely grated lime rind
  1 kaffir lime leaf, very finely
    shredded (optional)
  45ml/3 tbsp chopped chives or
    chopped chive flowers, plus extra
    chives or chive flowers to garnish
  2.5–5ml/½–1 tsp Thai fish sauce
  4 sole, skinned
  salt and ground black pepper
  lemon or lime wedges, to serve

COOK'S TIP
Finer white fish fillets, such as plaice,
can be cooked in this way, but reduce
the cooking time slightly.

1 Cream the butter with the lemon grass, lime rind, lime leaf, if using, and chives or chive flowers. Season to taste with Thai fish sauce, salt and pepper.

2 Chill the butter mixture to firm it a little, then form it into a roll and wrap in foil or clear film (plastic wrap). Chill until firm. Preheat the grill (broiler).

3 Brush the fish with melted butter. Place it on the grill rack and season. Grill (broil) for about 5 minutes on each side, until firm and just cooked.

4 Meanwhile, cut the chilled butter into thin slices and put these on the fish. Garnish with chives and serve with lemon or lime wedges.

Energy 349kcal/1447kJ; Protein 27.4g; Carbohydrate 0.5g, of which sugars 0.5g; Fat 26.3g, of which saturates 15g; Cholesterol 136mg; Calcium 49mg; Fibre 0g; Sodium 591mg

GRILLED HAKE WITH LEMON AND CHILLI

NOTHING COULD BE SIMPLER THAN PERFECTLY GRILLED FISH WITH A DUSTING OF CHILLI AND LEMON RIND. THIS IS AN IDEAL MEAL FOR THOSE OCCASIONS WHEN SOMETHING LIGHT IS CALLED FOR.

Preparation: 2 minutes; Cooking: 6–8 minutes

SERVES FOUR

INGREDIENTS
    4 hake fillets, each 150g/5oz
    30ml/2 tbsp olive oil
    finely grated rind and juice of
     1 lemon
    15ml/1 tbsp crushed chilli flakes
    salt and ground black pepper

VARIATION
Any firm white fish can be cooked in this simple, low-fat way. Try cod, halibut or hoki. If you haven't got any chilli flakes, brush the fish with chilli oil instead of olive oil.

1 Preheat the grill (broiler) to high. Brush the hake fillets all over with the olive oil and place them skin side up on a baking sheet.

2 Grill (broil) the fish for 4–5 minutes, until the skin is crispy, then carefully turn the fillets over in the pan, using a metal spatula.

3 Sprinkle the fillets with the lemon rind and chilli flakes and season with salt and ground black pepper.

4 Grill the fillets for a further 2–3 minutes, or until the hake is cooked through. (Test using the point of a sharp knife; the flesh should flake.) Squeeze over the lemon juice just before serving.

Energy 188kcal/786kJ; Protein 27g; Carbohydrate 0.1g, of which sugars 0.1g; Fat 8.8g, of which saturates 1.2g; Cholesterol 35mg; Calcium 22mg; Fibre 0g; Sodium 150mg

CHICKEN WITH LEMON AND GARLIC

CHICKEN STRIPS SPICED WITH PAPRIKA MAKE AN UNUSUAL COURSE FOR FOUR, AND ONLY NEED TO BE COOKED AT THE LAST MOMENT. SERVE THEM AS A MAIN COURSE WITH FRIED POTATOES.

Preparation: 3 minutes; Cooking: 3–5 minutes

SERVES TWO TO FOUR

INGREDIENTS
    2 skinless chicken breast fillets
    30ml/2 tbsp olive oil
    1 shallot, finely chopped
    4 garlic cloves, finely chopped
    5ml/1 tsp paprika
    juice of 1 lemon
    30ml/2 tbsp chopped fresh parsley
    salt and ground black pepper
    fresh flat leaf parsley, to garnish
    lemon wedges, to serve

VARIATION
For a variation on this dish, try using strips of turkey breast or pork fillet. They need slightly longer cooking. The whites of spring onions (scallions) can replace shallots, and the chopped green tops can be used instead of parsley.

1 Remove the little fillet from the back of each breast portion. If the breast still looks fatter than a finger, bat it with a rolling pin to make it thinner. Slice all the chicken meat into strips.

2 Heat the oil in a large frying pan. Stir-fry the chicken strips with the shallot, garlic and paprika over a high heat for about 3 minutes until cooked through.

3 Add the lemon juice and parsley and season with salt and pepper to taste. Serve hot with lemon wedges, garnished with flat leaf parsley.

COOK'S TIP
Chicken breasts have a little fillet strip that easily becomes detached. Collect these in a bag or container in the freezer for this dish.

Energy 139kcal/580kJ; Protein 18.6g; Carbohydrate 1.5g, of which sugars 1.1g; Fat 6.5g, of which saturates 1g; Cholesterol 53mg; Calcium 33mg; Fibre 0.8g; Sodium 50mg

FIERY CHICKEN WINGS WITH BLOOD ORANGES

THIS IS A GREAT RECIPE FOR THE BARBECUE — IT IS QUICK AND EASY, AND BEST EATEN WITH THE FINGERS. THE ORANGES CAN BE COOKED SEPARATELY OR WITH THE WINGS.

Preparation: 3 minutes; Cooking: 10 minutes

SERVES FOUR

INGREDIENTS
  60ml/4 tbsp fiery harissa
  30ml/2 tbsp olive oil
  16–20 chicken wings
  4 blood oranges, quartered
  icing (confectioners') sugar
  a small bunch of fresh coriander
    (cilantro), chopped
  salt

COOK'S TIP
Try making your own harissa if you have a blender. You will need 6–8 dried red chillies, 2 crushed garlic cloves, 2.5ml/ ½ tsp salt, 5ml/1 tsp ground cumin, 2.5ml/½ tsp ground coriander and 120ml/ 4fl oz/1 cup olive oil. Blend to a paste. To store, spoon into a jar and cover with olive oil. It will keep for 1 month.

1 Mix the harissa with the olive oil in a small bowl, or, if using home-made harissa, simply measure the required amount into a bowl. Add a little salt and stir to combine. Brush this mixture over the chicken wings so that they are well coated. Cook the wings on a hot barbecue or under a hot grill (broiler) for 5 minutes on each side.

2 Once the wings begin to cook, dip the orange quarters lightly in icing sugar and grill (broil) them for a few minutes, until they are slightly burnt but not blackened. If you thread them on to skewers, it will be easier to turn them under the heat. Serve the chicken wings immediately with the oranges, sprinkled with a little chopped fresh coriander.

Energy 658kcal/2758kJ; Protein 61.9g; Carbohydrate 21.8g, of which sugars 20.7g; Fat 36.7g, of which saturates 10.1g; Cholesterol 264mg; Calcium 163mg; Fibre 2.6g; Sodium 866mg

DUCK AND SESAME STIR-FRY

FOR A SPECIAL FAMILY MEAL THAT IS A GUARANTEED SUCCESS, THIS IS IDEAL. IT TASTES FANTASTIC AND COOKS FAST, SO YOU'LL BE EATING IN NO TIME.

Preparation: 3 minutes; Cooking: 5–7 minutes

SERVES FOUR

INGREDIENTS
    250g/9oz boneless duck meat
    15ml/1 tbsp sesame oil
    15ml/1 tbsp vegetable oil
    4 garlic cloves, finely sliced
    2.5ml/½ tsp dried chilli flakes
    15ml/1 tbsp Thai fish sauce
    15ml/1 tbsp light soy sauce
    120ml/4fl oz/½ cup water
    1 head broccoli, cut into small florets
    coriander (cilantro) and 15ml/1 tbsp
        toasted sesame seeds, to garnish

VARIATION
Pak choi (bok choy) or Chinese flowering cabbage can be used instead of broccoli.

1 Cut all the duck meat into bitesize pieces. Heat the oils in a wok or large, heavy frying pan and stir-fry the garlic over a medium heat until it is golden brown – do not let it burn. Add the duck to the pan and stir-fry for a further 2 minutes, until the meat begins to brown.

2 Stir in the chilli flakes, fish sauce, soy sauce and water. Add the broccoli and continue to stir-fry for about 2 minutes, until the duck is just cooked through.

3 Serve on warmed plates, garnished with coriander and sesame seeds.

Energy 165kcal/686kJ; Protein 17.4g; Carbohydrate 2.3g, of which sugars 2g; Fat 10.6g, of which saturates 1.8g; Cholesterol 69mg; Calcium 72mg; Fibre 2.9g; Sodium 345mg

STIR-FRIED DUCK WITH PINEAPPLE

THE FATTY SKIN ON DUCK MAKES IT IDEAL FOR STIR-FRYING: AS SOON AS THE DUCK IS ADDED TO THE HOT PAN THE FAT RUNS, CREATING DELICIOUS CRISP SKIN AND TENDER FLESH WHEN COOKED.

Preparation: 5 minutes; Cooking: 10 minutes

SERVES FOUR

INGREDIENTS
   250g/9oz fresh sesame noodles
   2 duck breasts, thinly sliced
   3 spring onions (scallions),
      cut into strips
   2 celery sticks, cut into
      matchstick strips
   1 fresh pineapple, peeled, cored and
      cut into strips
   300g/11oz carrots, peppers,
      beansprouts and cabbage, shredded
   90ml/6 tbsp plum sauce

1 Bring a pan of water to the boil and add the noodles. Cook for approximately 3 minutes then drain over the pan using a colander. Set aside.

2 Meanwhile, heat a wok. Add the sliced duck and stir-fry for 2 minutes, until slightly browned and crisp. Drain off all but 30ml/2 tbsp of the fat. Add the spring onions and celery and stir-fry for 2 minutes. Remove the ingredients from the wok and set aside.

3 Add the pineapple strips and mixed vegetables and stir-fry for 2 minutes.

4 Add the cooked noodles to the wok with the plum sauce and toss to combine, then replace the duck mixture.

5 Stir-fry the duck mixture for about 2 minutes more, or until the noodles and vegetables are hot and the duck is cooked through. Serve at once.

COOK'S TIP
Fresh sesame noodles can be bought from large supermarkets – you'll find them in the chiller cabinets alongside fresh pasta. If they aren't available use fresh egg noodles instead and cook according to the instructions on the packet. For extra flavour, add a little sesame oil to the cooking water.

Energy 455Kcal/1927kJ; Protein 28.3g; Carbohydrate 69g, of which sugars 22.6g; Fat 11g, of which saturates 1.4g; Cholesterol 110mg; Calcium 81mg; Fibre 5.7g; Sodium 143mg.

LAMB STEAKS WITH REDCURRANT GLAZE

GOOD AND MEATY, BUT THIN ENOUGH TO COOK QUICKLY, LAMB LEG STEAKS ARE A GOOD CHOICE FOR THE COOK SHORT ON TIME. THE REDCURRANT AND ROSEMARY GLAZE LOOKS GORGEOUS.

Preparation: 2–3 minutes; Cooking: 10 minutes

SERVES FOUR

INGREDIENTS
    4 large fresh rosemary sprigs
    4 lamb leg steaks
    75ml/5 tbsp redcurrant jelly
    30ml/2 tbsp raspberry or
    red wine vinegar

1 Reserve the tips of the rosemary and finely chop the remaining leaves. Rub the chopped rosemary, salt and pepper all over the lamb.

2 Preheat the grill (broiler). Heat the redcurrant jelly gently in a small pan with 30ml/2 tbsp water and a little seasoning. Stir in the vinegar.

3 Place the lamb steaks on a foil-lined grill (broiler) rack and brush with a little of the redcurrant glaze. Cook under the grill for about 5 minutes on each side, until deep golden, brushing frequently with more redcurrant glaze.

4 Transfer the lamb to warmed plates. Tip any juices from the foil into the remaining glaze and heat through gently. Pour the glaze over the lamb and serve, garnished with the reserved rosemary sprigs.

COOK'S TIP
This is a good recipe for the barbecue. Wait until the fierce heat has subsided and the coals are dusted with white ash, then place the rosemary-rubbed steaks directly on the grill rack. Brush frequently with the glaze as they cook. If you grow your own rosemary, try sprinkling some over the coals. As the oil in the herb warms, the scent of rosemary will perfume the air.

Energy 362kcal/1518kJ; Protein 34.4g; Carbohydrate 13g, of which sugars 13g; Fat 19.6g, of which saturates 9.1g; Cholesterol 133mg; Calcium 16mg; Fibre 0g; Sodium 156mg

LAMB'S KIDNEYS WITH MUSTARD SAUCE

THIS PIQUANT RECIPE IS SIMPLE AND FLEXIBLE, SO THE EXACT AMOUNTS OF ANY ONE INGREDIENT ARE UNIMPORTANT. IT MAKES A TASTY FIRST COURSE BUT WOULD BE EQUALLY SUITABLE AS A SUPPER DISH.

Preparation: 5 minutes; Cooking: 5 minutes

SERVES FOUR

INGREDIENTS

4–6 lamb's kidneys
butter, for frying
Dijon mustard or other mild mustard,
  to taste
250ml/8fl oz/1 cup white wine
5ml/1 tsp chopped fresh mixed
  herbs, such as rosemary, thyme,
  parsley and chives
1 small garlic clove, crushed
about 30ml/2 tbsp single
  (light) cream
salt and ground black pepper
fresh parsley, to garnish

COOK'S TIP
Look for kidneys that are firm, with a rich, even colour. Avoid those with dry spots or a dull surface.

1 Skin the kidneys and slice them horizontally. Remove the cores with scissors, and then wash them thoroughly in plenty of cold water. Drain and pat dry with kitchen paper.

2 Heat a little butter in a heavy frying pan and cook the kidneys for about 1½ minutes on each side. Be careful not to overcook. Remove the kidneys from the pan and keep warm.

3 Add a spoonful of mustard to the pan with the wine, herbs and garlic. Simmer gently to reduce the liquid by about half, then add enough cream to make a smooth sauce.

4 Return the kidneys to the pan and reheat gently in the sauce. Don't let them cook any further, or the kidneys will be tough. Serve garnished with parsley, and with rice or a green salad.

Energy 161kcal/675kJ; Protein 19.9g; Carbohydrate 0.6g, of which sugars 0.6g; Fat 4.4g, of which saturates 2g; Cholesterol 366mg; Calcium 22mg; Fibre 0g; Sodium 177mg

BARBECUED LAMB <u>WITH</u> RED PEPPER SALSA

VIBRANT RED PEPPER SALSA BRINGS OUT THE BEST IN SUCCULENT LAMB STEAKS TO MAKE A DISH THAT LOOKS AS GOOD AS IT TASTES. SERVE A SELECTION OF SALADS AND CRUSTY BREAD WITH THE LAMB.

Preparation: 3 minutes; Cooking: 4–10 minutes; Marinating for 24 hours recommended

SERVES SIX

INGREDIENTS

6 lamb steaks
about 15g/½oz/½ cup fresh
  rosemary sprigs
2 garlic cloves, sliced
60ml/4 tbsp olive oil
30ml/2 tbsp maple syrup
salt and ground black pepper
For the salsa
200g/7oz red (bell) peppers,
  roasted, peeled, seeded
  and chopped
1 garlic clove, crushed
15ml/1 tbsp chopped chives
30ml/2 tbsp extra virgin olive oil
fresh flat leaf parsley, to garnish

1 Place the lamb steaks in a dish and season with salt and pepper. Pull the leaves off the rosemary and sprinkle them over the meat.

2 Add the slices of garlic, then drizzle the olive oil and maple syrup over the top. Cover and chill until ready to cook. If you have time, the lamb can be left to marinate in the fridge for up to 24 hours.

3 Make sure the steaks are liberally coated with the marinating ingredients, then cook them over a hot barbecue for 2–5 minutes on each side. The cooking time depends on the heat of the barbecue coals and the thickness of the steaks as well as the result required – rare, medium or well cooked.

4 While the lamb steaks are cooking, mix together all the ingredients for the salsa in a bowl. Serve the salsa spooned on to the plates with the meat or in a small serving dish on the side. Garnish the lamb with sprigs of flat leaf parsley and serve with a cool, crisp salad – iceberg lettuce would be ideal.

Energy 390kcal/1627kJ; Protein 44.1g; Carbohydrate 2.1g, of which sugars 2g; Fat 22.8g, of which saturates 6.8g; Cholesterol 158mg; Calcium 33mg; Fibre 0.5g; Sodium 106mg

CUMIN- AND CORIANDER-RUBBED LAMB

WHEN SUMMER SIZZLES, TURN UP THE HEAT A LITTLE MORE WITH THESE SPICY LAMB CHOPS.
IF YOU HAVE TIME, MARINATE THE CHOPS FOR AN HOUR OR MORE — THEY WILL TASTE EVEN BETTER.
Preparation: 3 minutes; Cooking: 10 minutes. 1 hour's marinating time recommended

SERVES FOUR

INGREDIENTS
   30ml/2 tbsp ground cumin
   30ml/2 tbsp ground coriander
   30ml/2 tbsp olive oil
   8 lamb chops
   salt and ground black pepper

VARIATION
To make ginger- and garlic-rubbed pork, use pork chops instead of lamb chops and substitute the cumin and coriander with ground ginger and crushed garlic. Increase the cooking time to 7–8 minutes each side.

1 Prepare a barbecue or preheat the grill (broiler). Mix the cumin, coriander and oil in a bowl, beating with a spoon until a smooth paste is formed. Season with salt and pepper.

2 Rub the mixture all over the lamb chops. Cook the chops for 5 minutes on each side, until lightly charred on the outside but still pink in the centre. Serve immediately.

Energy 494kcal/2059kJ; Protein 55.6g; Carbohydrate 0g, of which sugars 0g; Fat 30.1g, of which saturates 12.6g; Cholesterol 220mg; Calcium 18mg; Fibre 0g; Sodium 150mg

PORK ON LEMON GRASS STICKS

THESE MAKE A SUBSTANTIAL SNACK, EITHER ON THEIR OWN OR AS PART OF A BARBECUE MENU. THE LEMON GRASS STICKS NOT ONLY ADD A SUBTLE FLAVOUR BUT ARE ALSO A GOOD TALKING POINT.

Preparation: 6 minutes; Cooking: 6–8 minutes

SERVES FOUR

INGREDIENTS

300g/11oz/1½ cups minced
  (ground) pork
4 garlic cloves, crushed
4 fresh coriander (cilantro) roots,
  finely chopped
2.5ml/½ tsp granulated sugar
15ml/1 tbsp soy sauce
salt and ground black pepper
8 x 10cm/4in lengths lemon
  grass stalk
sweet chilli sauce, to serve

VARIATION

Slimmer versions of these pork sticks are perfect for parties. The mixture will be enough for 12 lemon grass sticks if you use it sparingly.

1 Place the minced pork, crushed garlic, chopped coriander root, sugar and soy sauce in a large bowl. Season with salt and pepper to taste and mix well.

2 Divide into eight portions and mould each one into a ball. It may help to dampen your hands before shaping the mixture, to prevent it from sticking.

3 Stick a length of lemon grass halfway into each ball, then press the meat mixture around the lemon grass to make a shape like a chicken leg.

4 Cook the pork sticks under a hot grill (broiler) for 3–4 minutes on each side, until golden and cooked through. Serve with the chilli sauce for dipping.

Energy 132kcal/552kJ; Protein 14.7g; Carbohydrate 2g, of which sugars 1.6g; Fat 7.3g, of which saturates 2.7g; Cholesterol 50mg; Calcium 10mg; Fibre 0.2g; Sodium 317mg

PORK KEBABS WITH BBQ SAUCE

USE PORK FILLET FOR THESE KEBABS BECAUSE IT IS LEAN AND TENDER, AND COOKS VERY QUICKLY. THE KEBABS ARE GOOD SERVED WITH RICE, OR IN WARMED PITTA BREAD WITH LETTUCE.

Preparation: 3–4 minutes; Cooking: 10 minutes

SERVES FOUR

INGREDIENTS
    500g/1¼lb lean pork fillet
        (tenderloin)
    8 large, thick spring onions
        (scallions)
    120ml/4fl oz/½ cup barbecue sauce
    1 lemon

VARIATION
This is an unusual kebab recipe, in that the cubes of pork are only threaded on to the skewers after cooking. This is because the meat is regularly dipped in glaze, and it is easier to get an all-round coating if the cubes of pork are free. If you prefer to assemble the skewers first and cook them on the barbecue, do so. Use metal skewers that will not char, and baste frequently with the sauce.

1 Cut the pork into 2.5cm/1in cubes. Cut the spring onions into 2.5cm/1in-long sticks.

2 Preheat the grill (broiler) to high. Oil the wire rack and spread out the pork cubes on it. Grill (broil) the pork until the juices drip, then dip the pieces in the barbecue sauce and put back on the grill. Grill until cooked through, repeating the dipping process twice more. Set aside and keep warm.

3 Trim the spring onions and gently grill until soft and slightly brown on the outside. Do not dip in the barbecue sauce. Thread about four pieces of pork and three spring onion pieces on to each of eight bamboo skewers.

4 Arrange the skewers on a platter. Cut the lemon into wedges and squeeze a little lemon juice over each skewer. Serve immediately, offering the remaining lemon wedges separately.

Energy 192kcal/806kJ; Protein 27.6g; Carbohydrate 9.2g, of which sugars 8.8g; Fat 5.1g, of which saturates 1.8g; Cholesterol 79mg; Calcium 21mg; Fibre 0.6g; Sodium 578mg

WARM CHORIZO AND SPINACH SALAD

SPANISH CHORIZO SAUSAGE CONTRIBUTES AN INTENSE SPICINESS TO ANY INGREDIENT WITH WHICH IT IS COOKED. IN THIS HEARTY WARM SALAD, SPINACH HAS SUFFICIENT FLAVOUR TO COMPETE.

Preparation: 2–3 minutes; Cooking: 5 minutes

SERVES FOUR

INGREDIENTS
  225g/8oz baby spinach leaves
  90ml/6 tbsp extra virgin olive oil
  150g/5oz chorizo sausage, very
    thinly sliced
  30ml/2 tbsp sherry vinegar

VARIATION
Watercress or rocket (arugula) could be used instead of the spinach. For an added dimension use an oil flavoured with rosemary, garlic or chilli.

1 Discard any tough stalks from the spinach. Pour the oil into a large frying pan and add the sausage. Cook gently for 3 minutes, until the sausage slices start to shrivel slightly and begin to change colour.

2 Add the spinach leaves and remove the pan from the heat. Toss the spinach in the warm oil until it just starts to wilt. Add the sherry vinegar and a little seasoning. Toss the ingredients briefly, then serve immediately, while still warm.

Energy 300kcal/1238kJ; Protein 5.6g; Carbohydrate 4.5g, of which sugars 1.4g; Fat 29g, of which saturates 7g; Cholesterol 18mg; Calcium 111mg; Fibre 1.4g; Sodium 364mg

BEEF WITH BLUE CHEESE SAUCE

CELEBRATIONS CALL FOR SPECIAL DISHES, AND THIS ONE IS MORE SPECIAL THAN MOST. ROQUEFORT CHEESE, CREAM AND FILLET STEAK IS A RICH COMBINATION, SO KEEP THE REST OF THE MEAL SIMPLE.

Preparation: 2 minutes; Cooking: 8 minutes

SERVES FOUR

INGREDIENTS
  25g/1oz/2 tbsp butter
  30ml/2 tbsp olive oil
  4 fillet steaks, cut 5cm/2in thick,
    about 150g/5oz each
  salt and coarsely ground black pepper
  fresh flat leaf parsley, to garnish
For the blue cheese sauce
  30ml/2 tbsp brandy
  150ml/5fl oz/⅔ cup double
    (heavy) cream
  75g/3oz Roquefort cheese, crumbled

COOK'S TIP
Adding oil to the butter for frying means you can cook at a higher heat, essential for searing the meat.

1 Heat the butter and oil together in a heavy frying pan, over a high heat. Season the steaks well. Fry them for 1 minute on each side, to sear them.

2 Lower the heat slightly and cook for a further 2–3 minutes on each side, or according to your taste. Remove the steaks to a warm plate.

3 Reduce the heat and add the brandy, stirring to incorporate the pan juices. Add the cream and boil to reduce a little.

4 Add the crumbled cheese and mash it into the sauce using a spoon. Taste for seasoning. Serve in a small sauce jug (pitcher), or poured over the steaks. Garnish the beef with parsley.

Energy 573kcal/2374kJ; Protein 36.3g; Carbohydrate 0.7g, of which sugars 0.7g; Fat 45.4g, of which saturates 24.4g; Cholesterol 170mg; Calcium 117mg; Fibre 0g; Sodium 341mg

STEAK WITH WARM TOMATO SALSA

A TANGY SALSA OF TOMATOES, SPRING ONIONS AND BALSAMIC VINEGAR MAKES A COLOURFUL TOPPING FOR CHUNKY, PAN-FRIED STEAKS COOKED JUST THE WAY YOU LIKE THEM.

Preparation: 2–3 minutes; Cooking: 8 minutes

SERVES TWO

INGREDIENTS
- 2 steaks, about 2cm/¾in thick
- 3 large plum tomatoes
- 2 spring onions (scallions)
- 30ml/2 tbsp balsamic vinegar

1 Trim any excess fat from the steaks, then season on both sides with salt and pepper. Heat a non-stick frying pan and cook the steaks for about 3 minutes on each side for medium rare. Cook for a little longer if you like your steak well cooked.

2 Meanwhile, put the tomatoes in a heatproof bowl, cover with boiling water and leave for 1–2 minutes.

3 When the tomato skins start to split, drain and peel them, then halve them and scoop out the seeds. Dice the tomato flesh.

4 When the steaks are cooked to your taste, remove from the pan with a fish slice, to drain off any excess oil, and transfer them to plates. Keep the steaks warm on a very low oven temperature while you prepare the salsa.

5 Thinly slice the spring onions and add them to the cooking juices in the frying pan with the diced tomato, balsamic vinegar, 30ml/2 tbsp water and a little seasoning. Stir briefly until warm, scraping up any meat residue. Spoon the salsa over the steaks to serve.

COOK'S TIP

Choose rump, sirloin or fillet steak (beef tenderloin). If you prefer to grill (broil) the steak, the timing will be the same as in the recipe, although you must take into account the thickness of the meat.

Energy 207kcal/872kJ; Protein 33.9g; Carbohydrate 3.4g, of which sugars 3.4g; Fat 6.5g, of which saturates 2.7g; Cholesterol 89mg; Calcium 17mg; Fibre 1.2g; Sodium 100mg

PAN-FRIED STEAKS <u>WITH</u> WHISKY <u>AND</u> CREAM

A GOOD STEAK IS ALWAYS A POPULAR CHOICE FOR DINNER, AND TOP QUALITY MEAT PLUS TIMING ARE THE KEYS TO SUCCESS. CHOOSE SMALL, THICK STEAKS RATHER THAN LARGE, THIN ONES IF YOU CAN.

Preparation: 0 minutes; Cooking: 8 minutes

SERVES FOUR

INGREDIENTS

    4 x 225–350g/8–12oz sirloin steaks,
      at room temperature
    5ml/1 tsp oil
    15g/½oz/1 tbsp butter
    50ml/2fl oz/¼ cup Irish whiskey
    300ml/½ pint/1¼ cups double
      (heavy) cream
    salt and ground black pepper

1 Dry the steaks with kitchen paper and season with pepper. Heat a cast-iron frying pan, or other heavy pan, over high heat. When it is very hot, add the oil and butter. Add the steaks to the foaming butter, one at a time, to seal the meat quickly.

2 Lower the heat to moderate and continue to cook the steaks, allowing 3–4 minutes for rare, 4–5 minutes for medium or 5–6 minutes for well-done steaks.

3 To test if the timing is right, press down gently in the middle of the steak: soft meat will be rare; when there is some resistance but the meat underneath the outside crust feels soft, it is medium; if it is firm to the touch, the steak is well done.

COOK'S TIP

Turn the steaks only once during cooking to seal in the juices.

4 When the steaks are cooked to your liking, transfer them to warmed plates and keep warm. Pour off the fat from the pan and discard. Add the whiskey and stir around to scrape off all the sediment from the base of the pan.

5 Allow the liquid to reduce a little, then add the cream and simmer over a low heat for a few minutes, until the cream thickens. Season to taste, pour the sauce around or over the steaks, as you prefer, and serve immediately.

Energy 806kcal/3345kJ; Protein 65.9g; Carbohydrate 1.3g, of which sugars 1.3g; Fat 56.5g, of which saturates 32.6g; Cholesterol 251mg; Calcium 51mg; Fibre 0g; Sodium 232mg

VEGETARIAN DISHES

Vegetarian dishes are often praised for making innovative use of simple ingredients, and in a collection of quick dishes they are the stars. Their typical components – glowing vegetables, tasty grains, herbs and spices – are generally easy to prepare and cook. What's more, they tend not to cost a great deal, so you can afford to buy the best and still have change left over for some of life's luxuries, like a bottle of good wine or a punnet of strawberries for dessert. This chapter has a recipe for every occasion, from comforting nibbles such as Corn Fritters to ever-popular mains such as Mixed Bean and Tomato Chilli. Some dishes demand a bit of forward planning and a trip to the market or delicatessen; others require nothing more than a raid on the refrigerator and store cupboard or pantry. Spaghetti with Garlic and Oil, for instance, is as accessible as it sounds, with just six essential ingredients, all of which you are likely to have at hand. It is perfect for those occasions when even putting the kettle on seems to require too much effort, and can be on the table in less than a quarter of an hour.

CORN FRITTERS

SOMETIMES IT IS THE SIMPLEST DISHES THAT TASTE THE BEST. THESE FRITTERS, PACKED WITH CORN, ARE EASY TO PREPARE AND GO WELL WITH EVERYTHING FROM GAMMON TO NUT RISSOLES.

Preparation: 5 minutes; Cooking: 8 minutes

MAKES TWELVE

INGREDIENTS

3 corn cobs, total weight about
  250g/9oz
1 garlic clove, crushed
a small bunch of fresh coriander
  (cilantro), chopped
1 small fresh red or green chilli,
  seeded and finely chopped
1 spring onion (scallion),
  finely chopped
15ml/1 tbsp soy sauce
75g/3oz/¾ cup rice flour or plain
  (all-purpose) flour
2 eggs, lightly beaten
60ml/4 tbsp water
oil, for shallow-frying
salt and ground black pepper
sweet chilli sauce, to serve

1 Using a sharp knife, slice the kernels from the cobs using downward strokes. Rinse to remove any clinging debris from the cob and place in a bowl.

2 Add the garlic, chopped coriander, red or green chilli, spring onion, soy sauce, flour, beaten eggs and water to the corn and mix well. Season with salt and pepper to taste and mix again. The mixture should be firm enough to hold its shape, but not stiff.

3 Heat the oil in a large frying pan. Add spoonfuls of the corn mixture, gently spreading each one out with the back of the spoon to make a roundish fritter. Cook for 1–2 minutes on each side.

4 Drain the first batch of fritters on kitchen paper and keep hot on a foil-covered dish while frying more in the same way. Serve the fritters hot with sweet chilli sauce – arrange on a large plate around the sauce, if you like.

Energy 76kcal/314kJ; Protein 2.1g; Carbohydrate 7.6g, of which sugars 0.5g; Fat 4.1g, of which saturates 0.7g; Cholesterol 32mg; Calcium 14mg; Fibre 0.6g; Sodium 102mg

SESAME-TOSSED ASPARAGUS WITH NOODLES

TENDER ASPARAGUS SPEARS TOSSED WITH SESAME SEEDS AND SERVED ON A BED OF CRISPY, DEEP-FRIED NOODLES MAKES A LOVELY DISH FOR CASUAL ENTERTAINING.

Preparation: 2–3 minutes; Cooking: 7–8 minutes

SERVES FOUR

INGREDIENTS

15ml/1 tbsp sunflower oil
350g/12oz thin asparagus
    spears, trimmed
5ml/1 tsp salt
5ml/1 tsp ground black pepper
5ml/1 tsp golden caster
    (superfine) sugar
30ml/2 tbsp Chinese cooking wine
    or sherry
45ml/3 tbsp light soy sauce
60ml/4 tbsp vegetarian oyster sauce
10ml/2 tsp sesame oil
60ml/4 tbsp toasted sesame seeds
For the noodles
50g/2oz dried bean thread noodles
    or thin rice noodles
sunflower oil, for frying

1 First make the crispy noodles. Fill a wok one-third full of oil and heat to 180°C/350°F (or until a cube of bread, dropped into the oil, browns in 15 seconds). Add the noodles, small bunches at a time, to the oil; they will crisp and puff up in seconds. Using a slotted spoon, remove from the wok and drain on kitchen paper. Set aside.

COOK'S TIPS
• Vegetarian oyster sauce, made from dried mushrooms, is available from most supermarkets and Asian food stores. It is often labelled 'Mushroom oyster sauce'.
• Thin asparagus spears, called sprue, are often cheaper than fat stalks. Look for them at farmer's markets.

2 Heat a clean wok over a high heat and add the sunflower oil. Add the asparagus and stir-fry for 3 minutes.

3 Put four bowls to warm so that they are ready for serving.

4 Add the salt, pepper, sugar and wine or sherry to the wok with the soy sauce and oyster sauce. Stir-fry for 2–3 minutes. Add the sesame oil, toss to combine and remove from the heat.

5 To serve, divide the crispy noodles between four warmed plates or bowls and top with the asparagus and juices. Sprinkle over the toasted sesame seeds and serve immediately.

Energy 131kcal/547kJ; Protein 4.6g; Carbohydrate 16.5g, of which sugars 6.9g; Fat 5.6g, of which saturates 0.6g; Cholesterol 0mg; Calcium 31mg; Fibre 2g; Sodium 1047mg

GOAT'S CHEESE SALAD

YOU NEED A SOFT GOAT'S CHEESE WITH PLENTY OF FLAVOUR FOR THIS SALAD. IF YOU HAVE A GOOD CHEESE SHOP IN THE LOCALITY, MAKE A FRIEND OF THE OWNER AND ASK FOR SUGGESTIONS.

Preparation: 8–10 minutes; Cooking: 0 minutes

SERVES FOUR

INGREDIENTS
175g/6oz mixed salad leaves, such as
    lamb's lettuce, rocket (arugula),
    radicchio, frisée or cress
a few fresh large-leafed herbs, such
    as chervil and flat leaf parsley
15ml/1 tbsp toasted hazelnuts,
    roughly chopped
15–20 goat's cheese balls or cubes
For the dressing
30ml/2 tbsp hazelnut oil, olive oil
    or sunflower oil
5–10ml/1–2 tsp sherry vinegar or
    good wine vinegar, to taste
salt and ground black pepper

1 Tear up any large salad leaves. Put all the leaves into a large salad bowl with the fresh herbs and most of the toasted, chopped nuts (reserve a few for the garnish).

2 To make the dressing, whisk the hazelnut, olive or sunflower oil and vinegar together, and then season to taste with salt and pepper.

VARIATIONS
Toasted flaked (sliced) almonds could replace the hazelnuts (teamed with extra virgin olive oil), while stronger flavoured cheeses work well with walnuts and walnut oil.

3 Just before serving, toss the salad in the dressing and divide it among four serving plates. Arrange the drained goat's cheese balls or cubes over the leaves, sprinkle over the remaining chopped nuts and serve.

Energy 215kcal/893kJ; Protein 11.4g; Carbohydrate 1.5g, of which sugars 1.4g; Fat 18.3g, of which saturates 9.6g; Cholesterol 47mg; Calcium 84mg; Fibre 0.6g; Sodium 302mg

SALAD <u>OF</u> WILD GREENS <u>AND</u> OLIVES

THIS SIMPLE SALAD ONLY TAKES A FEW MINUTES TO PUT TOGETHER. USE AS WIDE A VARIETY OF GREENS AS YOU CAN FIND, MATCHING SWEET FLAVOURS WITH A FEW BITTER LEAVES FOR ACCENT.

Preparation: 6 minutes; Cooking: 0 minutes

SERVES FOUR

INGREDIENTS

   115g/4oz wild rocket (arugula)
   1 packet mixed salad leaves
   ¼ white cabbage, thinly sliced
   1 cucumber, sliced
   1 small red onion, chopped
   2–3 garlic cloves, chopped
   3–5 tomatoes, cut into wedges
   1 green (bell) pepper, seeded
    and sliced
   2–3 mint sprigs, sliced or torn
   15–30ml/1–2 tbsp chopped fresh
    parsley and/or tarragon or dill
   pinch of dried oregano or thyme
   45ml/3 tbsp extra virgin olive oil
   juice of ½ lemon
   15ml/1 tbsp red wine vinegar
   15–20 black olives
   salt and ground black pepper
   cottage cheese, to serve

1 In a large salad bowl, put the rocket, mixed salad leaves, sliced white cabbage, sliced cucumber, chopped onion and chopped garlic. Toss gently with your fingers to combine the leaves and vegetables.

COOK'S TIP
Try to find mixed salad leaves that include varieties such as lamb's lettuce, purslane and mizuna.

2 Arrange the tomatoes, pepper, mint, fresh and dried herbs, salt and pepper on top of the greens and vegetables. Drizzle over the oil, lemon juice and vinegar, stud with the olives and serve with a bowl of cottage cheese.

VARIATION
This is traditionally served with labneh or yogurt cheese, but tastes good with cottage cheese too.

Energy 150kcal/619kJ; Protein 3.3g; Carbohydrate 10.4g, of which sugars 9.8g; Fat 10.7g, of which saturates 1.6g; Cholesterol 0mg; Calcium 106mg; Fibre 4.2g; Sodium 338mg

LEMONY COUSCOUS SALAD

THIS POPULAR SALAD MIXES OLIVES, ALMONDS AND COURGETTES WITH FLUFFY COUSCOUS AND ADDS A HERB, LEMON JUICE AND OLIVE OIL DRESSING. IT HAS A DELICIOUSLY DELICATE FLAVOUR.

Preparation: 10 minutes; Cooking: 0 minutes

SERVES FOUR

INGREDIENTS

275g/10oz/1⅔ cups couscous
550ml/18fl oz/2½ cups boiling
  vegetable stock
2 small courgettes (zucchini)
16–20 black olives
25g/1oz/¼ cup flaked (sliced)
  almonds, toasted
60ml/4 tbsp olive oil
15ml/1 tbsp lemon juice
15ml/1 tbsp chopped fresh
  coriander (cilantro)
15ml/1 tbsp chopped fresh parsley
a good pinch of ground cumin
a good pinch of cayenne pepper

1 Place the couscous in a bowl and pour over the boiling stock. Stir with a fork and then set aside for 10 minutes until all the stock has been absorbed and the couscous has fluffed up.

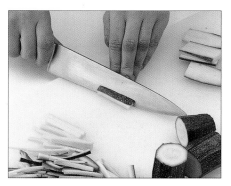

2 Meanwhile, trim the courgettes and cut them into pieces about 2.5cm/1in long. Slice into fine julienne strips with a sharp knife. Halve the black olives, discarding the stones (pits).

3 Fluff up the couscous with a fork, then carefully mix in the courgettes, olives and almonds.

4 Whisk the olive oil, lemon juice, coriander, parsley, cumin and cayenne in a bowl. Stir into the salad and toss gently. Transfer to a large serving dish and serve.

Energy 319kcal/1322kJ; Protein 6.6g; Carbohydrate 36.9g, of which sugars 1.4g; Fat 16.9g, of which saturates 2.1g; Cholesterol 0mg; Calcium 68mg; Fibre 1.8g; Sodium 286mg

AUBERGINE, MINT AND COUSCOUS SALAD

PACKETS OF FLAVOURED COUSCOUS ARE AVAILABLE IN MOST SUPERMARKETS — YOU CAN USE WHICHEVER YOU LIKE, BUT GARLIC AND CORIANDER IS PARTICULARLY GOOD FOR THIS RECIPE.

Preparation: 3 minutes; Cooking: 6 minutes

SERVES TWO

INGREDIENTS

1 large aubergine (eggplant)
30ml/2 tbsp olive oil
115g/4oz packet couscous flavoured
  with garlic and coriander (cilantro)
30ml/2 tbsp chopped fresh mint
salt and ground black pepper

VARIATION
For extra colour and flavour, add tomato to the salad. Grill (broil) about six baby plum tomatoes alongside the aubergine (eggplant).

1 Preheat the grill (broiler) to high. Cut the aubergine into large chunky pieces and toss them with the olive oil. Season with salt and pepper to taste and spread the aubergine pieces on a non-stick baking sheet. Grill (broil) for 5–6 minutes, turning occasionally, until golden brown.

2 Meanwhile, prepare the couscous according to the instructions on the packet.

3 Stir the grilled aubergine and chopped fresh mint into the garlic and coriander couscous, toss thoroughly and serve immediately.

Energy 251kcal/1044kJ; Protein 4.8g; Carbohydrate 32.5g, of which sugars 2g; Fat 12.1g, of which saturates 1.7g; Cholesterol 0mg; Calcium 53mg; Fibre 2g; Sodium 5mg

MIXED BEAN AND TOMATO CHILLI

THE ONLY TALENT THIS REQUIRES IS THE ABILITY TO OPEN A CAN, CHOP A CHILLI AND STIR A SAUCE.
IT'S IDEAL FOR THOSE DAYS WHEN YOUR ENERGY LEVELS ARE ZERO AND YOU NEED FOOD FAST.

Preparation: 2–3 minutes; Cooking: 12 minutes

SERVES FOUR

INGREDIENTS
   400g/14oz jar tomato and herb sauce
   2 x 400g/14oz cans mixed beans,
      drained and rinsed
   1 fresh red chilli
   a large handful of fresh coriander
      (cilantro)
   120ml/4fl oz/½ cup sour cream

1 Seed and thinly slice the chilli, then put it into a pan.

2 Pour the tomato sauce and mixed beans into a pan. Finely chop the fresh coriander. Set some aside for the garnish and add the remainder to the tomato and bean mixture. Stir the contents of the pan for a few seconds to mix all the ingredients together.

3 Bring the mixture to the boil, then quickly reduce the heat, cover and simmer gently for 10 minutes. Stir the mixture occasionally and add a dash of water if the sauce starts to dry out.

4 Ladle the chilli into warmed individual bowls and top with sour cream. Sprinkle with coriander and serve.

VARIATIONS
This chilli is great just as it is, served with chunks of bread, but you may want to dress it up a bit occasionally. Try serving it over a mixture of long grain and wild rice, piling it into split pitta breads or using it as a filling for baked potatoes. Serve with yogurt or crème fraîche instead of sour cream.

COOK'S TIP
Treat chillies with caution and wash your hands in soapy water after touching them. The capsaicin they contain is a powerful irritant and will cause eyes to sting if it comes into contact with them.

Energy 309kcal/1302kJ; Protein 16.7g; Carbohydrate 43.7g, of which sugars 14.1g; Fat 8.7g, of which saturates 4.2g; Cholesterol 18mg; Calcium 193mg; Fibre 12.4g; Sodium 1202mg

TOFU AND GREEN BEAN RED CURRY

THIS IS ONE OF THOSE VERSATILE RECIPES THAT SHOULD BE IN EVERY COOK'S REPERTOIRE. THIS
VERSION USES GREEN BEANS, BUT OTHER TYPES OF VEGETABLE WORK EQUALLY WELL.

Preparation: 2–3 minutes; Cooking: 7 minutes

SERVES FOUR TO SIX

INGREDIENTS
  600ml/1 pint/2½ cups canned
    coconut milk
  15ml/1 tbsp Thai red curry paste
  10ml/2 tsp palm sugar or honey
  225g/8oz/3¼ cups button
    (white) mushrooms
  115g/4oz/scant 1 cup green
    beans, trimmed
  175g/6oz firm tofu, rinsed, drained
    and cut into 2cm/¾ in cubes
  4 kaffir lime leaves, torn
  2 fresh red chillies, seeded
    and sliced
  fresh coriander (cilantro) leaves,
    to garnish

1 Pour about one-third of the coconut milk into a wok or pan. Cook until it starts to separate and an oily sheen appears on the surface.

2 Add the red curry paste and palm sugar or honey to the coconut milk. Mix thoroughly, then add the mushrooms. Stir and cook for 1 minute.

3 Stir in the remaining coconut milk. Bring back to the boil, then add the green beans and tofu cubes. Simmer gently for 4–5 minutes more.

4 Stir in the kaffir lime leaves and sliced red chillies. Spoon the curry into a serving dish, garnish with the coriander leaves and serve immediately.

Energy 59kcal/250kJ; Protein 3.8g; Carbohydrate 7.5g, of which sugars 7.1g; Fat 1.8g, of which saturates 0.4g; Cholesterol 0mg; Calcium 188mg; Fibre 0.8g; Sodium 291mg

SWEET AND SOUR VEGETABLES WITH TOFU

BIG, BOLD AND BEAUTIFUL, THIS IS A HEARTY STIR-FRY THAT WILL SATISFY THE HUNGRIEST GUESTS.
ONCE THE VEGETABLES ARE PREPARED, THEY TAKE ONLY MINUTES — IF NOT SECONDS — TO COOK.

Preparation: 6–8 minutes; Cooking: 5 minutes

SERVES FOUR

INGREDIENTS
4 shallots
3 garlic cloves
30ml/2 tbsp groundnut (peanut) oil
250g/9oz Chinese leaves (Chinese
  cabbage), shredded
8 baby corn cobs, sliced on
  the diagonal
2 red (bell) peppers, seeded and
  thinly sliced
200g/7oz/1¾ cups mangetouts
  (snow peas), trimmed and sliced
250g/9oz tofu, rinsed, drained and
  cut in 1cm/½ in cubes
60ml/4 tbsp vegetable stock
30ml/2 tbsp light soy sauce
15ml/1 tbsp granulated sugar
30ml/2 tbsp rice vinegar
2.5ml/½ tsp dried chilli flakes
small bunch coriander
  (cilantro), chopped

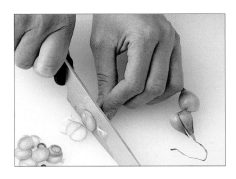

1 Slice the shallots thinly using a sharp knife. Finely chop the garlic.

2 Heat the oil in a wok or large frying pan and cook the shallots and garlic for 2–3 minutes over a medium heat, until golden. Do not let the garlic burn or it will taste bitter.

3 Add the shredded cabbage, toss over the heat for 30 seconds, then add the corn cobs and repeat the process.

4 Add the red peppers, mangetouts and tofu in the same way, each time adding a single ingredient and tossing it over the heat for about 30 seconds before adding the next ingredient.

5 Pour in the stock and soy sauce. Mix together the sugar and vinegar in a small bowl, stirring until the sugar has dissolved, then add to the wok or pan. Sprinkle over the chilli flakes and coriander, toss to mix well and serve.

Energy 180Kcal/751kJ; Protein 9.1g; Carbohydrate 17g, of which sugars 15.6g; Fat 8.7g, of which saturates 1.1g; Cholesterol 0mg; Calcium 386mg; Fibre 4.1g; Sodium 575mg.

STIR-FRIED CRISPY TOFU

VEGETARIAN GUESTS OFTEN DRAW THE SHORT STRAW AT DINNERS WHERE MEAT EATERS ARE IN THE MAJORITY. OFFER A DISH LIKE THIS ONE, AND THERE'LL BE ENVIOUS LOOKS FROM ACROSS THE TABLE.

Preparation: 3–4 minutes; Cooking: 10–12 minutes

SERVES ONE TO TWO

INGREDIENTS

- 250g/9oz deep-fried tofu cubes
- 30ml/2 tbsp groundnut (peanut) oil
- 15ml/1 tbsp Thai green curry paste
- 30ml/2 tbsp light soy sauce
- 2 kaffir lime leaves, rolled into cylinders and thinly sliced
- 30ml/2 tbsp granulated sugar
- 150ml/¼ pint/⅔ cup vegetable stock
- 250g/9oz asparagus, trimmed and sliced into 5cm/2in lengths
- 30ml/2 tbsp roasted peanuts, finely chopped

VARIATION

Substitute slim carrot batons, baby leeks or small broccoli florets for the asparagus, if you like.

1 Preheat the grill (broiler) to medium. Place the tofu cubes in a grill pan and grill (broil) for 2–3 minutes, then turn them over and continue to cook until they are crisp and golden brown all over. Watch them carefully; they must not be allowed to burn.

2 Heat the oil in a wok or heavy frying pan. Add the green curry paste and cook over a medium heat, stirring constantly, for 1–2 minutes, until it gives off its aroma.

3 Stir the soy sauce, lime leaves, sugar and vegetable stock into the wok or pan and mix well. Bring to the boil over a high heat, then reduce the heat to low so that the curried stock is just simmering. Do not allow the liquid to boil off, or the mixture will turn thick.

4 Add the asparagus and simmer gently for 5 minutes. Meanwhile, chop each piece of tofu into four, then add to the pan with the peanuts.

5 Toss the mixture thoroughly so that all the ingredients are coated in the sauce and warmed through, then spoon into a warmed dish and serve immediately.

Energy 551kcal/2287kJ; Protein 37.3g; Carbohydrate 7.8g, of which sugars 5.2g; Fat 41.4g, of which saturates 2.8g; Cholesterol 0mg; Calcium 1894mg; Fibre 3.1g; Sodium 1203mg

SESAME NOODLES

THIS IS ONE OF THOSE QUICK, COMFORTING DISHES THAT BECOME FAMILY FAVOURITES. CHILDREN LOVE ITS SWEET-SOUR FLAVOURS AND THERE ARE SHARP SPICES.

Preparation: 10 minutes; Cooking: 4 minutes

SERVES FOUR

INGREDIENTS

450g/1lb fresh egg noodles
½ cucumber, sliced lengthways,
   seeded and diced
4–6 spring onions (scallions)
a bunch of radishes, about 115g/4oz
225g/8oz mooli (daikon), peeled
115g/4oz/2 cups beansprouts, rinsed,
   then left in iced water and drained
60ml/4 tbsp groundnut (peanut) oil
   or sunflower oil
2 garlic cloves, crushed
45ml/3 tbsp toasted sesame paste
15ml/1 tbsp sesame oil
15ml/1 tbsp light soy sauce
5–10ml/1–2 tsp sweet chilli sauce,
   to taste
15ml/1 tbsp rice vinegar
120ml/4fl oz/½ cup vegetable stock
5ml/1 tsp sugar, or to taste
salt and ground black pepper
roasted cashew nuts, to garnish

1 Cook the fresh noodles in boiling water for 1 minute then drain well. Rinse the noodles in fresh water and drain again.

2 Place the cucumber in a colander or sieve (strainer), sprinkle with salt and leave to drain over a bowl for 10 minutes.

COOK'S TIP
Always check that guests do not have any nut allergies.

3 Meanwhile, cut the spring onions into fine shreds. Cut the radishes in half and slice finely. Coarsely grate the mooli. Rinse the cucumber, drain, pat dry and mix with all the vegetables in a salad bowl. Toss gently.

4 Heat half the oil in a wok or frying pan and stir-fry the noodles for about 1 minute. Using a slotted spoon, transfer the noodles to a large serving bowl and keep warm.

5 Add the remaining oil to the wok. When it is hot, fry the garlic to flavour the oil. Remove from the heat and stir in the sesame paste, with the sesame oil, soy and chilli sauces, vinegar and vegetable stock.

6 Add a little sugar and season to taste. Warm through but do not overheat. Pour the sauce over the noodles and toss well. Garnish with the cashew nuts and serve with the vegetables.

Energy 633kcal/2658kJ; Protein 17.6g; Carbohydrate 84.5g, of which sugars 5.3g; Fat 27.2g, of which saturates 5g; Cholesterol 34mg; Calcium 139mg; Fibre 5.7g; Sodium 484mg

SPAGHETTI WITH GARLIC AND OIL

IT DOESN'T GET MUCH SIMPLER THAN THIS: SPAGHETTI TOSSED WITH THE VERY BEST OLIVE OIL, WITH CHILLI FOR A HINT OF HEAT AND PLENTY OF PARSLEY FOR A CONTRASTING COOL, FRESH FLAVOUR.

Preparation: 1 minute; Cooking: 4–12 minutes

SERVES FOUR

INGREDIENTS

400g/14oz fresh or dried spaghetti
90ml/6 tbsp extra virgin olive oil
2–4 garlic cloves, crushed
1 dried red chilli
1 small handful fresh flat leaf
  parsley, roughly chopped
salt

1 Cook the pasta in a large pan of lightly salted boiling water. Dried pasta will take 10–12 minutes; fresh pasta about 3 minutes. Fresh pasta is ready when it rises to the surface of the water.

2 Meanwhile, heat the oil very gently in a small frying pan. Add the crushed garlic and whole dried chilli and stir over a low heat until the garlic is just beginning to brown. Remove the chilli and discard.

3 Drain the pasta and tip it into a warmed large bowl. Pour on the oil and garlic mixture, add the parsley and toss vigorously until the pasta glistens. Serve immediately in warm bowls.

COOK'S TIPS

• Since the oil is such an important ingredient here, only use the very best cold-pressed extra virgin olive oil.

• Don't use salt in the oil and garlic mixture, because it will not dissolve sufficiently. This is why salt is recommended for cooking the pasta.

• In Rome, grated Parmesan is never served with this dish, nor is it seasoned with pepper.

• In summer, Romans use fresh chillies, which they grow in pots on their terraces and window ledges. As the chilli is mainly used for flavouring, you could use chilli oil instead.

Energy 498kcal/2097kJ; Protein 12.6g; Carbohydrate 75.3g, of which sugars 3.4g; Fat 18.3g, of which saturates 2.6g; Cholesterol 0mg; Calcium 27mg; Fibre 3.2g; Sodium 3mg

FETTUCINE ALL'ALFREDO

THIS SIMPLE RECIPE WAS INVENTED BY A ROMAN RESTAURATEUR CALLED ALFREDO, WHO BECAME FAMOUS FOR SERVING IT WITH A GOLD FORK AND SPOON.

Preparation: 1–2 minutes; Cooking: 10–12 minutes

SERVES FOUR

INGREDIENTS
    50g/2oz/¼ cup butter
    200ml/7fl oz/scant 1 cup double
      (heavy) cream
    50g/2oz/⅔ cup freshly grated
      Parmesan cheese, plus
      extra to serve
    350g/12oz fresh fettucine

1 Melt the butter in a large pan. Add the cream and bring it to the boil. Simmer for 5 minutes, stirring constantly, then add the Parmesan cheese, with salt and freshly ground black pepper to taste, and turn off the heat under the pan.

2 Bring a large pan of salted water to the boil. Drop in the pasta all at once and quickly bring the water back to the boil, stirring occasionally. Cook the pasta for 2–3 minutes, or until it rises to the surface of the water and is tender. Drain well.

3 Turn on the heat under the pan of cream to low, add the cooked pasta all at once and toss until it is thoroughly coated in the sauce. Taste the sauce for seasoning. Serve immediately, with extra grated Parmesan cheese handed around separately.

Energy 697kcal/2912kJ; Protein 16.3g; Carbohydrate 65.8g, of which sugars 3.8g; Fat 42.8g, of which saturates 26g; Cholesterol 108mg; Calcium 199mg; Fibre 2.6g; Sodium 226mg

PANSOTTI WITH WALNUT SAUCE

WALNUTS, GARLIC OIL AND CREAM MAKE A STUNNINGLY SUCCESSFUL SAUCE FOR STUFFED PASTA. FOR SPEED AND FLAVOUR COOK WITH FRESH PASTA, NOW WIDELY AVAILABLE.

Preparation: 4 minutes; Cooking: 4–5 minutes

SERVES FOUR

INGREDIENTS

90g/3½oz/scant 1 cup shelled
 walnuts or walnut pieces
60ml/4 tbsp garlic-flavoured olive oil
120ml/4fl oz/½ cup double
 (heavy) cream
350g/12oz cheese and herb-filled
 pansotti or other stuffed pasta

1 Put the walnuts and garlic oil in a food processor and process to a paste, adding up to 120ml/4fl oz/½ cup warm water through the feeder tube to slacken the consistency. Spoon the mixture into a large bowl and add the cream. Beat well to mix, then season to taste with salt and black pepper.

2 Cook the pansotti or stuffed pasta in a large pan of salted boiling water for 4–5 minutes, or according to the instructions on the packet. Meanwhile, put the walnut sauce in a large warmed bowl and add a ladleful of the pasta cooking water to thin it.

3 Drain the pasta and tip it into the bowl of walnut sauce. Toss well, then serve immediately.

COOK'S TIP
Walnuts become rancid quite quickly, so you shouldn't store open packets in the pantry for long periods. For a sauce like this one, or anything else for which the walnuts are ground, buy the more economical walnut pieces.

VARIATION
Don't worry if you can't locate pansotti; tortellini will work just as well. The best place to buy the pasta for this recipe is a specialist deli where pasta is made on the premises.

Energy 702kcal/2931kJ; Protein 14.3g; Carbohydrate 66.1g, of which sugars 4g; Fat 44.1g, of which saturates 13g; Cholesterol 41mg; Calcium 58mg; Fibre 3.3g; Sodium 11mg

ON THE SIDE

Most vegetables benefit from being cooked in the shortest possible time, especially if they are young and tender. Their vibrant colours make any dish in which they feature look good, and there are so many varieties of vegetable that you can cook a different dish every night and never get bored. When you are in a hurry, it is better to cook just one vegetable accompaniment well, than to get all steamed up — both literally and figuratively — by trying to offer a selection. This chapter introduces some intriguing and innovative recipes, from Broccoli with Soy Sauce and Sesame Seeds to Turnip Salad in Sour Cream. There are hot and cold dishes in a range of textures, so you can choose whatever will best complement whatever else you are serving. For freshness and great taste, buy vegetables that have been grown close to where you live, from organic growers and farmer's markets if you can.

SAUTÉED HERB SALAD WITH CHILLI AND LEMON

FIRM-LEAFED FRESH HERBS, SUCH AS FLAT LEAF PARSLEY AND MINT TOSSED IN A LITTLE OLIVE OIL AND SEASONED WITH SALT, ARE FABULOUS WITH SPICY KEBABS OR STEAKS.

Preparation: 4–5 minutes; Cooking: 2 minutes

SERVES FOUR

INGREDIENTS

a large bunch of flat leaf parsley
a large bunch of mint
a large bunch of fresh
  coriander (cilantro)
a bunch of rocket (arugula)
a large bunch of spinach leaves,
  about 115g/4oz
60–75ml/4–5 tbsp olive oil
2 garlic cloves, finely chopped
1 fresh green or red chilli, seeded
  and finely chopped
½ preserved lemon, finely chopped
salt and ground black pepper
45–60ml/3–4 tbsp Greek
  (US strained plain) yogurt, to serve

1 Roughly chop the herbs and combine with the rocket and spinach. Heat the olive oil in a wide, heavy pan. Stir in the garlic and chilli, and fry until they begin to colour. Toss in the herbs and leaves and cook gently, until they begin to wilt.

2 Add the preserved lemon and season to taste. Serve warm with yogurt.

VARIATION
Flavour the yogurt with crushed garlic, if you like.

Energy 142kcal/585kJ; Protein 3.6g; Carbohydrate 3.1g, of which sugars 2.7g; Fat 12.9g, of which saturates 2.1g; Cholesterol 2mg; Calcium 216mg; Fibre 4.4g; Sodium 82mg

BROCCOLI <u>WITH</u> SOY SAUCE <u>AND</u> SESAME SEEDS

THE BEST WAY TO COOK BROCCOLI IS TO FRY IT QUICKLY IN A WOK, SO THAT THE RICH COLOUR AND CRUNCHY TEXTURE IS RETAINED. SOY SAUCE AND SESAME SEEDS ADD TO THE FLAVOUR.

Preparation: 2 minutes; Cooking: 3–4 minutes

SERVES TWO

INGREDIENTS
    225g/8oz purple sprouting broccoli
    15ml/1 tbsp sesame seeds
    15ml/1 tbsp olive oil
    15ml/1 tbsp soy sauce
    salt and ground black pepper

VARIATION
Purple sprouting broccoli has been used for this recipe. This vegetable is at its best when in season during early spring, so finding a good crop may not always be easy during the rest of the year. When it is not available, an ordinary variety of broccoli, such as calabrese, will also work very well. Or you could substitute the broccoli altogether for Chinese leaves, which offer just as much crunch.

1 Using a sharp knife, cut off and discard any thick stems from the broccoli and cut the broccoli into long, thin florets.

2 Spread out the sesame seeds in a small frying pan and dry-fry over a medium heat until toasted. Do not leave them unattended as they will readily burn if left just a fraction too long.

3 Heat the olive oil in a wok or large frying pan and add the broccoli. Stir-fry for 3–4 minutes, or until tender, adding a splash of water if the pan becomes too dry.

4 Add the soy sauce to the broccoli, then season with salt and ground black pepper to taste. Add sesame seeds, toss to combine and serve immediately.

Energy 135kcal/558kJ; Protein 6.6g; Carbohydrate 2.7g, of which sugars 2.3g; Fat 10.9g, of which saturates 1.7g; Cholesterol 0mg; Calcium 115mg; Fibre 3.5g; Sodium 545mg

BEETROOT WITH FRESH MINT

THE LOVELY, BRIGHT COLOUR OF BEETROOT CONTRASTS BEAUTIFULLY WITH THE DEEP GREEN OF MINT. THE FLAVOURS WORK WELL TOGETHER, TOO, AND ARE ENHANCED BY THE SWEET BALSAMIC DRESSING.

Preparation: 3–4 minutes; Cooking: 0 minutes; Chilling recommended

SERVES FOUR

INGREDIENTS
 4–6 cooked beetroot (beets)
 5–10ml/1–2 tsp sugar
 15–30ml/1–2 tbsp balsamic vinegar
 juice of ½ lemon
 30ml/2 tbsp extra virgin olive oil
 1 bunch fresh mint, leaves stripped
   and thinly sliced
 salt

VARIATIONS
• To make a spicy version, add harissa
to taste and substitute fresh coriander
(cilantro) for the mint.
• As an alternative, add a chopped onion
and some fresh dill.

1 Slice the beetroot or cut it into even-size dice with a sharp knife. Put the beetroot in a bowl. Add the sugar, balsamic vinegar, lemon juice, olive oil and a pinch of salt and toss together to combine.

2 Add half the thinly sliced fresh mint to the salad and toss lightly until well combined. If you have time, chill the salad for about 1 hour. Serve garnished with the remaining thinly sliced mint leaves.

Energy 90kcal/376kJ; Protein 1.9g; Carbohydrate 7.8g, of which sugars 6.7g; Fat 5.9g, of which saturates 0.8g; Cholesterol 0mg; Calcium 45mg; Fibre 1.2g; Sodium 69mg

CURRIED RED CABBAGE SLAW

THREE SHADES OF RED COMBINE IN THIS FRESH, CRISP SLAW. EACH CONTRIBUTES A DIFFERENT TEXTURE AND FLAVOUR, FROM THE CRUNCH OF CABBAGE TO THE SATIN SMOOTHNESS OF PEPPER.

Preparation: 5 minutes; Cooking: 0 minutes; Chilling recommended

SERVES FOUR TO SIX

INGREDIENTS
  ½ red cabbage, thinly sliced
  1 red (bell) pepper, chopped
    or very thinly sliced
  ½ red onion, chopped
  60ml/4 tbsp red or white wine
    vinegar or cider vinegar
  60ml/4 tbsp sugar, or to taste
  120ml/4fl oz/½ cup Greek
    (US strained plain) yogurt or
    natural (plain) yogurt
  120ml/4fl oz/½ cup mayonnaise,
    preferably home-made
  1.5ml/¼ tsp curry powder
  2–3 handfuls raisins
  salt and ground black pepper

1 Put the cabbage, pepper and red onion in a bowl and toss to combine. In a small pan, heat the vinegar and sugar until the sugar has dissolved, then pour over the vegetables. Leave to cool slightly.

2 Combine the yogurt and mayonnaise, then mix into the cabbage mixture. Season to taste with curry powder, salt and ground black pepper, then mix in the raisins.

3 Chill the salad before serving, if you have time. Just before serving, drain off any excess liquid and briefly stir the slaw again.

VARIATION
If you prefer, ready-made low-fat mayonnaise can be used instead of the Greek yogurt and mayonnaise mixture. Stir the curry powder into the mayonnaise.

Energy 272kcal/1136kJ; Protein 3g; Carbohydrate 27.9g, of which sugars 27.5g; Fat 17.5g, of which saturates 3.4g; Cholesterol 15mg; Calcium 74mg; Fibre 2g; Sodium 120mg

STIR-FRIED BRUSSELS SPROUTS <u>WITH</u> BACON

THIS IS A GREAT WAY OF COOKING BRUSSELS SPROUTS, HELPING TO RETAIN THEIR SWEET FLAVOUR
AND CRUNCHY TEXTURE. STIR-FRYING GUARANTEES THAT THERE WILL NOT BE A SINGLE SOGGY SPROUT.

Preparation: 4 minutes; Cooking: 5 minutes

SERVES FOUR

INGREDIENTS
   450g/1lb Brussels sprouts, trimmed
    and washed
   30ml/2 tbsp sunflower oil
   2 streaky (fatty) bacon rashers
    (strips), finely chopped
   10ml/2 tsp caraway seeds,
    lightly crushed
   salt and ground black pepper

COOK'S TP
Save time on preparation by buying
diced bacon or diced pancetta, available
ready-packaged at the supermarket,
which needs no further preparation.
Just tip it straight into the pan.

1 Using a sharp knife, carefully cut all
the Brussels sprouts into fine shreds.

2 Heat the oil in a wok or large frying
pan. Add the shredded sprouts and turn
quickly over the heat, season with salt
and ground black pepper, then remove
and set aside.

3 Use the the same wok or pan to cook
the chopped bacon. Stir-fry for 1–2
minutes until golden.

4 Return the seasoned sprouts to the
pan containing the bacon and stir in the
caraway seeds. Cook for a further 1–2
minutes, then serve immediately.

Energy 131kcal/545kJ; Protein 5.9g; Carbohydrate 4.6g, of which sugars 3.5g; Fat 10g, of which saturates 2g; Cholesterol 8mg; Calcium 30mg; Fibre 4.6g; Sodium 164mg

STIR-FRIED CARROTS <u>WITH</u> MANGO <u>AND</u> GINGER

RIPE, SWEET MANGO TASTES WONDERFUL WITH CARROTS AND GINGER IN THIS SPICY VEGETABLE DISH, WHICH IS GOOD ENOUGH TO SERVE ON ITS OWN WITH YOGURT AND A SALAD.

Preparation: 6 minutes; Cooking: 4–5 minutes

SERVES FOUR TO SIX

INGREDIENTS

15–30ml/1–2 tbsp olive oil

2–3 garlic cloves, chopped

1 onion, chopped

25g/1oz fresh root ginger, peeled
and chopped

5–6 carrots, sliced

30–45ml/2–3 tbsp shelled pistachio
nuts, roasted

5ml/1 tsp ground cinnamon

5–10ml/1–2 tsp ras el hanout

1 small firm, ripe mango, peeled and
coarsely diced

a small bunch of fresh coriander
(cilantro), finely chopped

juice of ½ lemon

salt

1 Heat the olive oil in a heavy frying pan or wok. Stir in the garlic, then the onion and ginger. Fry for 1 minute. Add the carrots, tossing them in the pan to make sure that they are mixed with the flavouring ingredients, and cook until they begin to brown.

2 Add the roasted pistachio nuts, ground cinnamon and ras el hanout, then gently mix in the diced mango. Sprinkle with the finely chopped fresh coriander, season with salt and pour over the lemon juice. Toss to mix and serve immediately.

Energy 89kcal/371kJ; Protein 1.7g; Carbohydrate 8.2g, of which sugars 7.5g; Fat 5.7g, of which saturates 0.8g; Cholesterol 0mg; Calcium 23mg; Fibre 2.2g; Sodium 47mg

CAULIFLOWER <u>WITH</u> EGG <u>AND</u> LEMON

ALTHOUGH CAULIFLOWER HAS SHRUGGED OFF ITS IMAGE AS THE VEGETABLE MOST PEOPLE LOVE TO HATE, IT STILL NEEDS A BIT OF A MAKEOVER NOW AND THEN.

Preparation: 2–3 minutes; Cooking: 12 minutes

SERVES FOUR

INGREDIENTS
75–90ml/5–6 tbsp extra virgin
  olive oil
1 medium cauliflower, divided into
  large florets
2 eggs
juice of 1 lemon
5ml/1 tsp cornflour (cornstarch),
  mixed to a cream with a little
  cold water
30ml/2 tbsp chopped fresh flat
  leaf parsley
salt

VARIATION
This delightful, summery style of cooking cauliflower is popular in the Mediterranean. It works equally well with a close relative, broccoli. Divide the broccoli into small florets and cook for slightly less time than the cauliflower, until just tender.

1 Heat the olive oil in a large heavy pan, add the cauliflower florets and sauté over a medium heat until they start to brown.

2 Pour in enough hot water to almost cover the cauliflower, add salt to taste, then cover the pan and cook for 7–8 minutes until the florets are just soft. Remove the pan from the heat and leave to stand, covered, while you make the sauce.

3 Beat the eggs in a bowl, add the lemon juice and cornflour and beat until mixed. Beat in a few tablespoons of the hot liquid from the cauliflower.

4 Pour the egg mixture slowly over the cauliflower, then stir gently. Place the pan over a very gentle heat for 2 minutes to thicken the sauce, but do not allow to boil. Spoon into a warmed serving bowl, sprinkle with parsley and serve.

Energy 201kcal/833kJ; Protein 7g; Carbohydrate 4.4g, of which sugars 2.7g; Fat 17.5g, of which saturates 3g; Cholesterol 95mg; Calcium 51mg; Fibre 2.2g; Sodium 47mg

TURNIP SALAD IN SOUR CREAM

OFTEN NEGLECTED, TURNIPS MAKE AN UNUSUAL AND VERY TASTY ACCOMPANIMENT WHEN PREPARED IN THIS SIMPLE WAY. CHOOSE YOUNG, TENDER TURNIPS OF THE TYPE THE FRENCH CALL NAVETS.

Preparation: 5 minutes; Cooking: 0 minutes

SERVES FOUR

INGREDIENTS

2–4 young, tender turnips, peeled
¼–½ onion, finely chopped
2–3 drops white wine vinegar,
   or to taste
60–90ml/4–6 tbsp sour cream
salt and ground black pepper
chopped fresh parsley or paprika,
   to garnish

VARIATION
Crème fraîche or thick yogurt can be used instead of the sour cream, if you like.

1 Thinly slice or coarsely grate the turnips. Alternatively, thinly slice half the turnips and grate the ones that remain. Put in a bowl.

2 Add the onion, vinegar, salt and pepper, toss together then stir in the sour cream. Serve chilled, garnished with a sprinkling of parsley or paprika.

Energy 48kcal/198kJ; Protein 1.1g; Carbohydrate 4.1g, of which sugars 3.7g; Fat 3.2g, of which saturates 1.9g; Cholesterol 9mg; Calcium 42mg; Fibre 1.4g; Sodium 14mg

HOT AND CHILLED DESSERTS

You may not want to serve something sweet every day, but there are times when nothing succeeds like a Cool Chocolate Float. Or for a truly speedy dessert, whip up a Blueberry Meringue Crumble. Both these treats are blitzed in the blender before being served in tall glasses and are classy and cool. On the lighter side of hot home-made puddings, try Summer Berries in Warm Sabayon Glaze or Passion Fruit Soufflés, which will make a fitting conclusion to a rich or spicy main course. Fruit and cheese are always a winning combination, and you'll find two trimphant dinner party pleasers here in the shape of Pears with Blue Cheese and Walnuts. Some of the recipes in this chapter benefit from being made ahead of time. The unashamedly indulgent Chocolate and Prune Refrigerator Bars fall into that category, but they will also keep for several days and make perfect portable snacks.

RHUBARB AND GINGER TRIFLES

CHOOSE A GOOD QUALITY JAR OF RHUBARB COMPOTE FOR THIS RECIPE; TRY TO FIND ONE WITH LARGE, CHUNKY PIECES OF FRUIT. ALTERNATIVELY, USE WHOLE-FRUIT APRICOT JAM.

Preparation: 3–4 minutes; Cooking: 0 minutes

SERVES FOUR

INGREDIENTS
12 gingernut biscuits (gingersnaps)
50ml/2fl oz/¼ cup rhubarb compote
450ml/¾ pint/scant 2 cups extra
   thick double (heavy) cream

1 Put the ginger biscuits in a plastic bag and seal. Bash the biscuits with a rolling pin until roughly crushed.

2 Set aside two tablespoons of crushed biscuits and divide the rest among four glasses.

3 Spoon the rhubarb compote on top of the crushed biscuits, then top with the cream. Place in the refrigerator and chill for about 30 minutes.

4 To serve, sprinkle the reserved crushed biscuits over the trifles and serve immediately.

Energy 695kcal/2874kJ; Protein 3.6g; Carbohydrate 27.1g, of which sugars 14.1g; Fat 64.3g, of which saturates 39.4g; Cholesterol 154mg; Calcium 98mg; Fibre 0.6g; Sodium 124mg

CHOCOLATE ᴬⁿᵈ PRUNE REFRIGERATOR BARS

WICKEDLY SELF-INDULGENT AND VERY EASY TO MAKE, THESE FRUITY CHOCOLATE BARS WILL KEEP FOR 2–3 DAYS IN THE REFRIGERATOR — IF THEY DON'T ALL GET EATEN AS SOON AS THEY ARE READY.

Preparation: 4 minutes; Cooking: 0 minutes; Chilling recommended

MAKES TWELVE BARS

INGREDIENTS
    250g/9oz good quality
      milk chocolate
    50g/2oz/¼ cup unsalted
      (sweet) butter
    115g/4oz digestive biscuits
      (graham crackers)
    115g/4oz/½ cup ready-to-eat prunes

1 Break the chocolate into small pieces and place in a heatproof bowl. Add the butter and melt in the microwave on high for 1–2 minutes. Stir to mix and set aside. (Alternatively, place the chocolate pieces in a bowl over a pan of gently simmering water and leave until melted, stirring frequently.)

2 Put the biscuits in a plastic bag and seal, then bash into small pieces with a rolling pin. Alternatively, break up the biscuits in a food processor but do not let them become too fine. Use the pulse button. Roughly chop the prunes and stir into the melted chocolate with the biscuits.

3 Spoon the chocolate and prune mixture into a 20cm/8in square cake tin (pan) and smooth away any lumps and bumps with the back of the spoon. Chill for 1–2 hours until set. Remove the cake from the refrigerator and, using a sharp knife, cut into 12 bars of about 1.5cm/½ in thickness each.

Energy 197kcal/826kJ; Protein 2.5g; Carbohydrate 21.7g, of which sugars 16.4g; Fat 11.8g, of which saturates 6.8g; Cholesterol 18mg; Calcium 59mg; Fibre 0.9g; Sodium 102mg

BLUEBERRY MERINGUE CRUMBLE

IMAGINE THE MOST APPEALING FLAVOURS OF A BLUEBERRY MERINGUE DESSERT — FRESH TANGY FRUIT, CRISP SUGARY MERINGUE AND PLENTY OF VANILLA-SCENTED CREAM, ALL SERVED IN A TALL GLASS FOR EASY EATING

Preparation: 4 minutes; Cooking: 0 minutes

SERVES THREE TO FOUR

INGREDIENTS

150g/5oz/1¼ cups fresh blueberries,
  plus extra to decorate
15ml/1 tbsp icing
  (confectioners') sugar
250ml/8fl oz/1 cup vanilla
  iced yogurt
200ml/7fl oz/scant 1 cup full cream
  (whole) milk
30ml/2 tbsp lime juice
75g/3oz meringues, lightly crushed

1 Put the blueberries and sugar in a blender or food processor with 60ml/4 tbsp water and blend until smooth, scraping the mixture down from the side once or twice, if necessary.

2 Transfer the purée to a small bowl and rinse out the blender or food processor bowl to get rid of any remaining blueberry juice.

3 Put the iced yogurt, milk and lime juice in the blender and process until thoroughly combined. Add half of the crushed meringues and process again until smooth.

4 Carefully pour alternate layers of the milkshake, blueberry syrup and the remaining crushed meringues into tall glasses, finishing with a few chunky pieces of meringue.

5 Drizzle any remaining blueberry syrup over the tops of the meringues and decorate with a few extra blueberries. Serve immediately.

COOK'S TIPS

• Buy good-quality meringues, not the brittle extra-sweet supermarket variety.
• The easiest way to crush the meringues is to put them in a plastic bag on a work surface and tap them gently with a rolling pin. Stop tapping the meringues as soon as they have crumbled into little bitesize pieces otherwise you'll just be left with tiny crumbs.

VARIATION

Iced yogurt is used to provide a slightly lighter note than ice cream, but there's nothing to stop you using ice cream instead.

Energy 164kcal/691kJ; Protein 6.2g; Carbohydrate 30.8g, of which sugars 30.8g; Fat 2.7g, of which saturates 1.6g; Cholesterol 8mg; Calcium 197mg; Fibre 1.2g; Sodium 96mg

COOL CHOCOLATE FLOAT

CHOCOLATE MILKSHAKE AND SCOOPS OF CHOCOLATE AND VANILLA ICE CREAM ARE COMBINED HERE TO MAKE THE MOST MELTINGLY DELICIOUS DESSERT DRINK EVER. IT'S CLASS IN A GLASS.

Preparation: 6 minutes; Cooking: 2 minutes

SERVES TWO

INGREDIENTS
   115g/4oz plain (semisweet)
      chocolate, broken into pieces
   250ml/8fl oz/1 cup milk
   15ml/1 tbsp caster (superfine) sugar
   4 large scoops classic vanilla
      ice cream
   4 large scoops dark (bittersweet)
      chocolate ice cream
   a little lightly whipped cream
   grated chocolate or chocolate curls,
      to decorate

4 Using a dessertspoon, drizzle the chocolate milk over and around the ice cream in each glass, so that it dribbles down in swirls.

5 Top with lightly whipped cream and sprinkle over a little grated chocolate or some chocolate curls to decorate. Serve immediately.

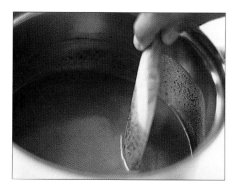

1 Put the chocolate in a heavy pan and add the milk and sugar. Heat gently, stirring with a wooden spoon until the chocolate has melted and the mixture is smooth. Pour into a bowl and set in a larger bowl of iced water to cool quickly.

2 Blend the cooled chocolate mixture with half of the ice cream in a blender or food processor until the mixture resembles chocolate milk.

3 Scoop the remaining ice cream alternately into two tall glasses: vanilla then chocolate.

COOK'S TIP
You can experiment with all kinds of flavours of ice cream. Try substituting banana, coconut or toffee flavours for the chocolate and vanilla ice cream if you prefer. The health-conscious cook might prefer to substitute frozen yogurt, but make sure it is a creamy variety.

Energy 990kcal/4149kJ; Protein 17.7g; Carbohydrate 115.4g, of which sugars 110.4g; Fat 52.3g, of which saturates 32g; Cholesterol 83mg; Calcium 518mg; Fibre 1.5g; Sodium 262mg

PEARS <u>WITH</u> BLUE CHEESE <u>AND</u> WALNUTS

SUCCULENT PEARS FILLED WITH BLUE CHEESE AND WALNUT CREAM ARE A WONDERFUL SWEET-SAVOURY COMBINATION. OMIT THE GARNISH OF LEAVES IF YOU THINK THIS WILL MAKE THE DISH TOO HEAVY.

Preparation: 8–10 minutes; Cooking: 0 minutes

SERVES SIX

INGREDIENTS
  115g/4oz fresh cream cheese
  75g/3oz Stilton or other mature blue
    cheese, such as Roquefort
  30–45ml/2–3 tbsp single
    (light) cream
  115g/4oz/1 cup roughly
    chopped walnuts
  6 ripe pears
  15ml/1 tbsp lemon juice
  sea salt and ground black pepper
  optional: mixed salad leaves,
    such as frisée, oakleaf lettuce
    and radicchio, to garnish
  walnut halves and sprigs of fresh
    flat leaf parsley, to garnish
For the dressing
  juice of 1 lemon
  a little finely grated lemon rind
  a pinch of caster (superfine) sugar
  60ml/4 tbsp olive oil

2 Peel and halve the pears and scoop out the core from each. Put the pears into a bowl of water with the 15ml/ 1 tbsp lemon juice to prevent them from browning. Make the dressing by whisking the ingredients together with salt and pepper to taste.

3 Arrange a bed of salad leaves on six plates – shallow soup plates are ideal – add a cherry tomato to each and sprinkle over the remaining chopped walnuts.

4 Drain the pears well and pat dry with kitchen paper, then turn them in the prepared dressing and arrange, hollow side up, on the plate or, if preferred, on the mixed leaf garnish.

5 Divide the blue cheese filling among the 12 pear halves and spoon the dressing over the top. Garnish each filled pear half with a walnut half and a sprig of flat leaf parsley before serving.

1 Mash the cream cheese and blue cheese together in a mixing bowl with a good grinding of black pepper, then blend in the cream to make a smooth mixture. Add 25g/1oz/¼ cup of the chopped walnuts and mix to distribute evenly.

COOK'S TIP
You need small pears that are perfectly ripe for this recipe. Comice or Bartlett pears would be ideal.

Energy 322kcal/1332kJ; Protein 5.1g; Carbohydrate 15.7g, of which sugars 15.7g; Fat 26.9g, of which saturates 10.2g; Cholesterol 30mg; Calcium 109mg; Fibre 3.7g; Sodium 218mg

CUSTARD-FILLED NECTARINES

STEAMING NECTARINES OR PEACHES BRINGS OUT THEIR NATURAL SWEETNESS, AND THIS IS A QUICK AND EASY WAY OF MAKING THE MOST OF LEFT-OVER FRUIT THAT ISN'T QUITE AS RIPE AS IT COULD BE.

Preparation: 5 minutes; Cooking: 5–10 minutes

SERVES FOUR TO SIX

INGREDIENTS
   6 nectarines
   1 large (US extra large) egg
   45ml/3 tbsp palm sugar or light
     muscovado (brown) sugar
   30ml/2 tbsp coconut milk

COOK'S TIP
Palm sugar, also known as jaggery, is made from the sap of certain Asian palm trees, such as coconut and palmyrah. It is available from Asian food stores. If you buy it as a cake or large lump, you need to grate it before use. Muscovado sugar makes a good substitute as it has a similar, toffee-like flavour.

1 Cut the nectarines in half. Using a teaspoon, scoop out the stones (pits) and hollow out smoothly by removing a little of the surrounding flesh.

2 Lightly beat the egg, then add the sugar and the coconut milk. Beat until the sugar has dissolved.

3 Transfer the nectarines to a steamer and pour the custard mixture into each of the cavities, filling them about three-quarters full. Steam the filled halves over a pan of simmering water for 5–10 minutes. Remove from the heat and leave to cool completely before transferring to plates and serving.

Energy 213kcal/897kJ; Protein 12.6g; Carbohydrate 21.6g, of which sugars 21.6g; Fat 9.4g, of which saturates 2.6g; Cholesterol 317mg; Calcium 64mg; Fibre 1.8g; Sodium 124mg.

ZABAGLIONE

LIGHT AS AIR AND HIGHLY ALCOHOLIC, THIS WARM CUSTARD IS A MUCH-LOVED ITALIAN PUDDING.
IT IS TRADITIONALLY MADE WITH MARSALA, BUT MADEIRA OR SWEET SHERRY CAN BE USED INSTEAD.

Preparation: 8 minutes; Cooking: 5–7 minutes

2 Gradually add the Marsala, Madeira or sherry to the egg mixture, 15ml/ 1 tbsp at a time, whisking well after each addition.

3 Place the bowl over a pan of gently simmering water and continue to whisk for 5–7 minutes, until the mixture becomes thick; when the beaters are lifted they should leave a thick trail on the surface of the mixture. Do not be tempted to underbeat the mixture, as the zabaglione will be too runny and will be likely to separate.

4 Pour into four warmed, stemmed glasses and serve immediately with amaretti for dipping.

SERVES FOUR

INGREDIENTS
   4 egg yolks
   50g/2oz/¼ cup caster
      (superfine) sugar
   60ml/4 tbsp Marsala, Madeira or
      sweet sherry
   amaretti, to serve

VARIATION
To make a chocolate version of this dessert, whisk in 30ml/2 tbsp unsweetened cocoa powder with the wine or sherry and serve dusted with cocoa powder and icing (confectioners') sugar.

1 Place the egg yolks and sugar in a large heatproof bowl, and whisk with an electric beater until the mixture is pale and has thickened considerably.

COOK'S TIP
Zabaglione is also delicious served as a sauce with cooked fruit. Try serving it with poached pears, grilled (broiled) peaches or baked bananas to create a really special dessert.

Energy 131kcal/548kJ; Protein 3g; Carbohydrate 14.1g, of which sugars 14.1g; Fat 5.5g, of which saturates 1.6g; Cholesterol 202mg; Calcium 31mg; Fibre 0g; Sodium 12mg

PINEAPPLE AND RUM CREAM

WHEN PINEAPPLE IS HEATED, THE FLAVOUR INTENSIFIES AND THE GORGEOUS SWEET JUICES CARAMELIZE. ADD RUM AND CREAM AND YOU HAVE A DREAM OF A DESSERT.

Preparation: 4 minutes; Cooking: 4 minutes

SERVES FOUR

INGREDIENTS
    25g/1oz/2 tbsp butter
    115g/4oz pineapple, roughly chopped
    45ml/3 tbsp dark rum
    300ml/½ pint/1¼ cups double
      (heavy) cream

VARIATIONS
Although a sumptuous dessert in its own right, this fruity alcoholic cream also works very well as a topping. Spoon over vanilla or rum-and-raisin ice cream for an extra special touch to a simple dessert. Peach slices, apple rings or halved bananas can also be used instead of pineapple pieces, if you prefer.

1 Heat the butter in a frying pan and add the pineapple. Cook over a moderate to high heat until the pineapple is starting to turn golden.

2 Add the rum and allow to bubble for 1–2 minutes, then remove and set aside. Pour the cream into a bowl and beat until soft. Fold the pineapple and rum mixture evenly through the cream, then spoon carefully into four glasses and serve immediately.

Energy 455kcal/1876kJ; Protein 1.4g; Carbohydrate 4.2g, of which sugars 4.2g; Fat 45.5g, of which saturates 28.3g; Cholesterol 116mg; Calcium 43mg; Fibre 0.4g; Sodium 55mg

CHOCOLATE AND BANANA FOOL

THIS DELICIOUS DESSERT HAS A LOVELY CITRUS FLAVOUR. IT IS QUITE RICH, SO IT IS A GOOD IDEA TO SERVE IT WITH SOME DESSERT COOKIES, SUCH AS SHORTBREAD OR BISCOTTI.

Preparation: 3 minutes; Cooking: 2 minutes; Chilling recommended

SERVES FOUR

INGREDIENTS
  115g/4oz plain (semisweet)
    chocolate, broken into
    small pieces
  300ml/½ pint/1¼ cups ready-made
    fresh custard
  2 bananas

COOK'S TIPS
Good quality bought custard is ideal for this dessert. Don't be tempted to use anything but the best chocolate, though, or the flavour will be compromised. Look for a bar that contains at least 70 percent chocolate solids. A flavoured chocolate such as pistachio or orange takes the dessert into another dimension.

1 Put the chocolate pieces in a heat-proof bowl and melt in the microwave on high power for 1–2 minutes. Stir, then set aside. If you do not have a microwave, put the chocolate in a heatproof bowl and place it over a pan of gently simmering water and leave until melted, stirring frequently to remove any unmelted pieces.

2 Pour the custard into a bowl and gently fold in the melted chocolate to make a rippled effect.

3 Peel and slice the bananas and stir these into the chocolate and custard mixture. Spoon into four glasses. If you have time, chill for at least 30 minutes before serving.

Energy 268kcal/1127kJ; Protein 4.1g; Carbohydrate 42.1g, of which sugars 38.1g; Fat 9.6g, of which saturates 4.9g; Cholesterol 3mg; Calcium 81mg; Fibre 1.4g; Sodium 33mg

LEMON POSSET

THIS OLD-FASHIONED DESSERT WAS ONCE CONSIDERED A REMEDY FOR THE COMMON COLD. IT IS CERTAINLY WORTH SUFFERING A SNIFFLE IF IT MEANS YOU GET TO SAMPLE ITS SUPERB FLAVOUR.

Preparation: 2 minutes; Cooking: 8–10 minutes; Chilling recommended

SERVES FOUR

INGREDIENTS
  600ml/1 pint/2½ cups double
    (heavy) cream
  175g/6oz/scant 1 cup caster
    (superfine) sugar
  grated rind and juice of
    2 unwaxed lemons

VARIATION
To intensify the lemon flavour of this lovely old dessert even more, swirl a spoonful of lemon curd or lemon cheese on the surface just before serving. Physalis make a suitable and very stylish accompaniment.

1 Pour the cream into a heavy pan. Add the sugar and heat gently until the sugar has dissolved, then bring to the boil, stirring constantly. Add the lemon juice and rind, reserving a little of the rind for decoration, and stir constantly over a medium heat until it thickens.

2 Pour the mixture into four heatproof serving glasses. Cool, then chill in the refrigerator until just set. Serve the posset decorated with a few strands of lemon rind, and with a selection of dessert biscuits (cookies), if you like. Rich, buttery shortbread is ideal.

Energy 917kcal/3801kJ; Protein 2.7g; Carbohydrate 48.5g, of which sugars 48.5g; Fat 80.6g, of which saturates 50.1g; Cholesterol 206mg; Calcium 98mg; Fibre 0g; Sodium 36mg

Summer Berries in Warm Sabayon Glaze

This luxurious combination consists of summer berries under a light and fluffy sauce flavoured with liqueur. The topping is lightly grilled to form a crisp, caramelized crust.

Preparation: 9 minutes; Cooking: 2 minutes

SERVES FOUR

INGREDIENTS

    450g/1lb/4 cups mixed summer
      berries, or soft fruit

    4 egg yolks

    50g/2oz/¼ cup vanilla sugar or
      caster (superfine) sugar

    120ml/4fl oz/½ cup liqueur, such as
      Cointreau, kirsch or Grand Marnier,
      or a white dessert wine

    a little icing (confectioners') sugar,
      sifted, and mint leaves, to decorate
      (optional)

COOK'S TIP

If you prefer to omit the alcohol, use grape, mango or apricot juice.

1 Arrange the fruit in four heatproof ramekins. Preheat the grill (broiler).

2 Whisk the yolks in a large bowl with the sugar and liqueur or wine. Place over a pan of hot water and whisk constantly until thick, fluffy and pale.

3 Pour equal quantities of the sauce into each dish. Place under the grill for 1–2 minutes until just turning brown. Dust the fruit with icing sugar and sprinkle with mint leaves just before serving, if you like. You could also add an extra splash of liqueur.

Energy 235kcal/984kJ; Protein 3.9g; Carbohydrate 27.1g, of which sugars 27.1g; Fat 5.6g, of which saturates 1.6g; Cholesterol 202mg; Calcium 48mg; Fibre 1.3g; Sodium 18mg

SYRUPY BRIOCHE SLICES WITH ICE CREAM

KEEP A FEW INDIVIDUAL BRIOCHE BUNS IN THE FREEZER TO MAKE THIS SUPER DESSERT. FOR A SLIGHTLY TARTER TASTE, USE FINELY GRATED LEMON RIND AND JUICE INSTEAD OF ORANGE RIND.

Preparation: 4 minutes; Cooking: 9–10 minutes

SERVES FOUR

INGREDIENTS
  butter, for greasing
  finely grated rind and juice of
    1 orange, such as Navelina or
    blood orange
  50g/2oz/¼ cup caster
    (superfine) sugar
  90ml/6 tbsp water
  1.5ml/¼ tsp ground cinnamon
  4 brioche buns
  15ml/1 tbsp icing
    (confectioners') sugar
  400ml/14fl oz/1⅔ cups vanilla
    ice cream

1 Lightly grease a gratin dish and set aside. Put the orange rind and juice, sugar, water and cinnamon in a heavy pan. Heat gently, stirring constantly, until the sugar has dissolved, then boil rapidly, without stirring, for 2 minutes, until thickened and syrupy.

2 Remove the orange syrup from the heat and pour it into a shallow heatproof dish. Preheat the grill (broiler). Cut each brioche vertically into three thick slices. Dip one side of each slice in the hot syrup and arrange in the gratin dish, syrupy sides down. Reserve the remaining syrup. Grill (broil) the brioche until lightly toasted.

VARIATION
Substitute the same amount of ground cardamom for the cinnamon.

3 Using tongs, turn the brioche slices over and dust well with icing sugar. Grill for about 3 minutes more, or until they are just beginning to caramelize around the edges.

4 Transfer the hot brioche to serving plates and top with scoops of vanilla ice cream. Spoon the remaining syrup over them and serve immediately.

COOK'S TIP
You could also use slices of a larger brioche, rather than buns, or madeleines, sliced horizontally in half. These are traditionally flavoured with lemon or orange flower water, making them especially tasty.

Energy 399kcal/1681kJ; Protein 8.5g; Carbohydrate 65.5g, of which sugars 42.5g; Fat 12g, of which saturates 7.2g; Cholesterol 25mg; Calcium 174mg; Fibre 1.3g; Sodium 252mg

PINEAPPLE BAKED ALASKA

NO MATTER HOW MANY TIMES YOU MAKE THIS CLASSIC PUDDING, YOU'LL ALWAYS MARVEL AT HOW THE
ICE CREAM STAYS COLD UNDER ITS MERINGUE JACKET, EVEN AFTER ITS ENCOUNTER WITH A HOT OVEN.

Preparation: 5 minutes; Cooking: 5–7 minutes

SERVES THREE TO FOUR

INGREDIENTS

   3 large egg whites
   150g/5oz/¾ cup caster
     (superfine) sugar
   25g/1oz/⅓ cup desiccated (dry
     unsweetened shredded) coconut
   175–225g/6–8oz piece ready-made
     cake, such as ginger or chocolate
   6 slices ripe, peeled pineapple
   500ml/17fl oz/2 cups vanilla ice
     cream, in a brick
   a few cherries or figs, to decorate

1 Preheat the oven to 230°C/450°F/
Gas 8. Whisk the egg whites in a
grease-free bowl until stiff, then whisk
in the sugar until the mixture is stiff and
glossy. Fold in the coconut.

2 Slice the cake into two thick layers
the same rectangular shape as the ice
cream. Cut the pineapple into triangles
or quarters, cutting it over the cake to
catch any drips. On a baking sheet,
arrange the fruit on top of one slice of
cake. Top with the ice cream and then
the second layer of cake.

3 Spread the meringue over the cake
and ice cream, and bake in the oven for
5–7 minutes, or until turning golden.
Serve immediately, topped with fruit.

COOK'S TIP
Do not use soft-scoop ice cream for this
dessert as it will soften too quickly.

Energy 667kcal/2808kJ; Protein 10.8g; Carbohydrate 104.6g, of which sugars 93.9g; Fat 25.7g, of which saturates 9.9g; Cholesterol 33mg; Calcium 215mg; Fibre 2.3g; Sodium 317mg

FRUIT-FILLED SOUFFLÉ OMELETTE

THIS IMPRESSIVE DISH IS SURPRISINGLY QUICK AND EASY TO MAKE. THE CREAMY OMELETTE FLUFFS UP IN THE PAN, FLOPS OVER TO ENVELOP ITS FRUIT FILLING AND THEN SLIDES ON TO THE PLATE.

Preparation: 5 minutes; Cooking: 4–5 minutes

SERVES TWO

INGREDIENTS
  75g/3oz/¾ cup strawberries, hulled
  45ml/3 tbsp kirsch, brandy
    or Cointreau
  3 eggs, separated
  30ml/2 tbsp caster (superfine) sugar
  45ml/3 tbsp double (heavy)
    cream, whipped
  a few drops of vanilla extract
  25g/1oz/2 tbsp butter
  icing (confectioners') sugar, sifted

1 Cut the strawberries in half and place in a bowl. Pour over 30ml/2 tbsp of the liqueur and set aside to macerate.

2 Beat the egg yolks and sugar together until pale and fluffy, then fold in the whipped cream and vanilla extract. Whisk the egg whites until stiff, then carefully fold in the yolks.

COOK'S TIP
You can give your omelette a professional look by marking sizzling grill lines on top. Protecting your hand with an oven glove, hold a long, wooden-handled skewer directly over a gas flame until it becomes very hot and changes colour. Sprinkle the top of the omelette with icing sugar, then place the hot skewer on the sugar, which will caramelize very quickly. Working quickly, before the skewer becomes too cold to caramelize the sugar, make as many lines as you like.

3 Melt the butter in an omelette pan. When sizzling, pour in the egg mixture and cook until set underneath, shaking occasionally. Spoon on the strawberries and liqueur and, tilting the pan, slide the omelette so that it folds over.

4 Carefully slide the omelette on to a warm serving plate, spoon over the remaining liqueur, and serve dredged with icing sugar. Cut the omelette in half, transfer to two warmed plates and eat immediately.

Energy 434kcal/1802kJ; Protein 10.2g; Carbohydrate 18.4g, of which sugars 18.4g; Fat 30.7g, of which saturates 16.4g; Cholesterol 343mg; Calcium 70mg; Fibre 0.4g; Sodium 189mg

PASSION FRUIT SOUFFLÉS

IF YOU SHUN SOUFFLÉS BECAUSE YOU IMAGINE THEM TO BE DIFFICULT, TRY THESE DELIGHTFULLY EASY DESSERTS BASED ON BOUGHT CUSTARD. THEY ARE GUARANTEED TO RISE TO THE OCCASION.

Preparation: 3–4 minutes; Cooking: 8–10 minutes

SERVES FOUR

INGREDIENTS
200ml/7fl oz/scant 1 cup ready-made fresh custard
3 passion fruits
2 egg whites
softened butter, for greasing

1 Preheat the oven to 200°C/400°F/ Gas 6. Grease four 200ml/7fl oz/scant 1 cup ramekin dishes with the butter.

COOK'S TIP
Run the tip of the spoon handle around the inner rim of the soufflé mixture in each ramekin before baking to ensure even rising.

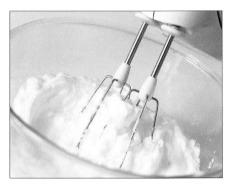

2 Pour the custard into a large mixing bowl. Cut the passion fruits in half. Using a teaspoon, carefully scrape out the seeds and juice from the halved passion fruit so that they drop straight on to the custard. Beat the mixture with a metal spoon until well combined, and set aside.

3 Whisk the egg whites until stiff, and fold a quarter of them into the custard. Carefully fold in the remaining egg whites, then spoon the mixture into the ramekin dishes. Place the dishes on a baking sheet and bake for 8–10 minutes, or until the soufflés are well risen. Serve immediately.

Energy 59kcal/249kJ; Protein 3.1g; Carbohydrate 8.8g, of which sugars 7.1g; Fat 1g, of which saturates 0g; Cholesterol 1mg; Calcium 48mg; Fibre 0.4g; Sodium 53mg

CHOCOLATE HAZELNUT GALETTES

THIS STUNNING DESSERT DOESN'T REQUIRE ANY COOKING, BUT YOU DO NEED TO ALLOW TIME FOR THE CHOCOLATE TO SET. IT MAKES AN IMPRESSIVE FINALE FOR A SOPHISTICATED DINNER PARTY.

Preparation: 10–12 minutes; Cooking: 0 minutes; Chilling recommended

SERVES FOUR

INGREDIENTS
175g/6oz plain (semisweet)
  chocolate, broken into squares
45ml/3 tbsp single (light) cream
30ml/2 tbsp flaked (sliced) hazelnuts
115g/4oz white chocolate, broken
  into squares
175g/6oz/¾ cup fromage frais
  or mascarpone
15ml/1 tbsp dry sherry
60ml/4 tbsp finely chopped
  hazelnuts, toasted
physalis, dipped in white chocolate,
  to decorate

1 Melt the chocolate in a small heatproof bowl over a pan of just-boiled water, then remove from the heat and stir in the cream.

2 Draw 12 x 7.5cm/3in circles on sheets of baking parchment. Turn the paper over and spread the chocolate and cream mixture over each marked circle, covering in a thin, even layer. Sprinkle flaked hazelnuts over four of the circles, then leave to set.

3 Melt the white chocolate in a heatproof bowl over just-boiled water, then stir in the fromage frais or mascarpone and dry sherry. Fold in the chopped, toasted hazelnuts. Leave to cool until the mixture holds its shape.

4 Remove the chocolate rounds carefully from the paper and sandwich them together in stacks of three, spooning the hazelnut cream between each layer and using the hazelnut-covered rounds on top. Chill for around half an hour before serving, if possible.

5 To serve, place the galettes on individual plates and decorate with chocolate-dipped physalis.

VARIATION
Use almonds instead of hazelnuts if you prefer, and add a drop or two of almond extract to the fromage frais or mascarpone mixture.

COOK'S TIP
The chocolate could be spread over heart shapes instead, for a special Valentine's Day dessert.

Energy 597kcal/2489kJ; Protein 10.7g; Carbohydrate 48.1g, of which sugars 47.2g; Fat 41.1g, of which saturates 17.5g; Cholesterol 13mg; Calcium 182mg; Fibre 2.6g; Sodium 55mg

INDEX